THE BATTLE OF BRITAIN MEMORIAL FLIGHT

RICHARD WINSLADE

FOREWORD BY SQN LDR AL PINNER MBE

SUTTON PUBLISHING

First published in the United Kingdom in 2007 by
Sutton Publishing Limited · Phoenix Mill
Thrupp · Stroud · Gloucestershire · GL5 2BU

Copyright © Richard Winslade, 2007

Richard Winslade has asserted the moral right to be identified as
the author of this work.

British Library Cataloguing in Publication Data
A catalogue record for this book is available from the British
Library.

ISBN 978-0-7509-3151-9

Typeset in 10/13.5 pt Sabon.
Typesetting and origination by
Sutton Publishing Limited.
Printed and bound in England.

TECHNICAL INFORMATION

The camera equipment used to photograph the Flight for this book is as follows.

Air-to-air photography with the Flight during the early days was with Nikon F and F2 35mm SLR cameras using 20mm, 55mm and 85mm lenses. More recently I have been using an Asahi Pentax 637 medium format camera with 45mm, 105mm and 165mm lenses.

All engineering photography has been carried out with a Mamiya RB67 using 65mm, 90mm and 185mm lenses.

The film used for the 35mm cameras was Kodachrome X (64 ISO), and for the medium format equipment, Fujichrome Provia RDP 100.

Contents

I dedicate this book to my wife Susan, who has been unstinting in her support; also to my son Ollie, who has only a passing interest in aeroplanes (his particular passion is trains so, clearly, further education is needed); and to my daughter Lucy, who is interested in neither but has managed to keep me almost sane over the years.

On a more serious note, I also dedicate this book to those who gave their lives during the Second World War. They were all someone's dearest person.

Foreword

Sqn Ldr Al Pinner MBE, OC BBMF

It was during my Chipmunk conversion in late 2002, prior to my first season on the Flight, that I met Richard Winslade. On first impression he is a charming, mild-mannered and watchful man and it is probably this last quality which has stood him in such great stead as a photographer. Yes, he captures some wonderful aerial shots, but he also achieves some incredibly dramatic pictures of men working on machinery. These classic shots illustrate the engineers' passion for their work and their consummate skill in maintaining these priceless pieces of national heritage in airworthy condition; it is the engineers who are the reason behind the Flight's enduring success.

Richard has been photographing the Flight for longer than I have been in the RAF and he relates stories of the varied characters that have flown and worked on the Flight over the years. Just recently, I took him up in a Chipmunk to photograph the Dakota and our other Chipmunk for this book. Shortly after we got airborne, the Dakota became unserviceable and we were faced with a twenty-minute delay. Poor Richard had the window out of the rear cockpit on a cold dank January day, yet he regaled me with such tales that we could have whiled away several hours waiting for the other aircraft. (Incidentally, it is no wonder that the 'Major' has contributed so much to this book since most of the tales concern him!)

The other Chipmunk duly arrived and we climbed through a gap in the clouds into brilliant sunshine. Richard took two shots and declared himself happy. By the time the Dakota arrived the gaps had all but closed up and we had to make the best of the lacklustre conditions. We spotted one ray of light in the Lincolnshire sky and motored towards it. Two minutes later Richard declared 'Got it!' and we were complete. It is the mark of his talent behind the lens that without the benefit of the preview screen on the back of a digital camera, he knew that the shot was in the can – truly a master of his craft.

Richard has been a tremendous friend and champion of the Flight and his superb photography has served to keep us firmly in the public eye. This lovely book is very much a personal account of his long association with the Flight, beautifully illustrated with his remarkable photographs – truly a labour of love. We at the Flight hope that you thoroughly enjoy this book and we remain very grateful to Richard for his time, his enthusiasm and his continued and generous support.

Al Pinner
RAF Coningsby, March 2007

Prologue

Sqn Ldr Paul Day OBE, AFC, RAF (Retd)

OC BBMF, 1996–2003

It is now more than two decades since I worked with Richard Winslade on his previous book about the Battle of Britain Memorial Flight, way back in the early to mid-1980s when I had hair and teeth and faculties. Even so, I should have been more on my guard against his blandishments that I contribute the prologue to this one. I have written a few others in my time, and it would seem that all authors share the same interesting traits: they all seem to want attention in September (BBMF's busiest month) and they all promise 'detailed résumés' of their books' contents to ease the burden. Richard Winslade's detailed résumé consisted of an e-mail addressed to someone else – and intercepted entirely by chance – which stated '750–1000 words, pronto' followed by some excruciating smarm. *Plus ça change*!

It is to the changes the Flight has undergone since I joined it in 1980 that I will address the majority of this Prologue, starting with the equipment changes, most of which will be common knowledge among air-minded readers. Our support aircraft, Devon VP981, was replaced by Dakota ZA947 in 1993, the Devon subsequently being sold in 1997 to Air Atlantique, in whose historic collection it still flies. Spitfire XIX PS853 was sold in 1994 to defray the cost of the rebuilding of Hurricane LF363, which crash-landed at Wittering in 1991 and returned to BBMF service in 1998; PS853 still flies the circuit under Rolls-Royce ownership. A second Chipmunk, WG486, joined WK518 in 1995 after long service at RAF Gatow in Berlin, and two years later in 1997 Spitfire IX MK356 joined the Flight, after rebuild, from the RAF St Athan Collection. These 'above-surface' changes have maintained the status quo in the fighter fleet and greatly increased our training and support capability. The status of the Dakota as a true historic aircraft (as opposed to support only) is something of a two-edged sword, but in general it increases our display capability and adds para-dropping to our repertoire.

The 'below-surface' changes have been of equal if not greater significance. Over the winter of 1996–7 the Lancaster was given a new main spar, which should ensure an airframe life of another fifty years or so, which bodes well for the future. A long-standing problem with the lack of available hangar-floor spare engines came to a head in 1999 when the fighter fleet was reduced to a single Griffon Spitfire by early August, most other engines having been 'donated' to keep the Lancaster flying. The problem was not lack of engines per se: we owned upwards of ten Merlins, but they were all un-inspected and un-refurbished and therefore as efficacious as mammaries on a mackerel. I am sure that David Heatherington and Don McLeod would reject the epithet of unsung heroes, David at that time having engineering and financial responsibility for the Flight as Nimrod Project Team Leader, and Don having served as our Support Manager for many years. Nevertheless, as a result of David's inspired direction and financial management and Don's inside knowledge and arduous leg-work, combined with a serendipitous introduction to Retro Track and Air of Dursley, Gloucestershire, who now refurbish our Rolls-Royce V12s, the Flight now has shop-floor spares of all five types ready to go at a moment's notice. Further, it is entirely to the credit of the same two gentlemen that the ex-Exhibition Flight Mk XVI Spitfires were acquired for the Flight in 2002 – a *much* more difficult acquisition than is generally recognised. Within a very short time one of the Merlin 66s from the Mk XVIs was fulfilling its purpose in the no. 3 spot of the Lancaster and, as I write, most major components either have been refurbished as on-the-shelf spares or are in the process of becoming so. The current incumbents of the Nimrod Team continue to offer their support unstintingly; for many years the Flight has held a plethora of spares (hangars-full, even) which have remained uncategorised and in some cases unidentified, often stored in less than ideal conditions and in some cases in remote locations. Under a current initiative all that will end. Coningsby will become the single point of storage in purpose-built units, with proper categorisation.

And so to personnel. Eight years as Commanding Officer persuaded me that the lucky bastard who fills that spot is of minimal importance. I say that having taken over from my predecessor at virtually no notice right at the kick-off to the 1996 season and at nobody's particular choice; it was simply that I was in the right place at the right time. With very little interference from me either then or since, the Flight has run smoothly from year to year under an ever-increasing demand for its services, as any well-constituted military organisation should. However, I consider it indicative of a brighter future that my successor – and his successor too – were nominated and their tenures stated well in advance.

Other aircrew are not so straightforward, thanks mainly to a 30 per cent drawdown of the front line since the end of the Cold War, very little reduction in commitment (not just one but two Gulf Wars) and the continuation of spare-time BBMF status. We continue to field a highly professional team by casting the net wider, our 'heavies' now being crewed by volunteers from AWACs, Jetstream and Dominie; and our fighters by Tornado F3 and Harrier pilots. We also have on board our second female aircrew as Loadmaster on the Dakota, having long fielded female engineers.

However, it was at the start of the millennium that the real personnel crisis reared its head in engineering. The air force said goodbye to its last big piston, the Shackleton, in 1993 and the Flight soldiered on by relying on the last of those who had seen service on similar types and by the dubious expedient of dedicated tradesmen declining postings and in some cases promotion to extend their love affair with 'real' engineering. This is no way to run a railway, and it flies particularly badly with other halves who only partially share the enthusiasm and must have one eye at least on children's education, provision for the future and other such mundane irrelevancies. Matters came to a head when it became apparent that were the Engine Trade Manager to leave on promotion, his replacement would never even have seen a piston engine of any description, let alone a Rolls-Royce V12.

I recall this as an attention-grabbing moment which had cascade effects throughout the Engine and

Airframe trades, and to a lesser degree through Electronics and Avionics. We were urgently in need of a solution. That solution was provided by the transfer of Regular air force personnel to Full Time Reserve status, thus removing key players from the jeopardy of postings, promotions and detached duties and ensuring their long-term tenure and the Flight's engineering future. Combined with this innovation is the recognition that the best (and only) lead-in training for BBMF is BBMF itself, which in turn has led to the establishment of a Training Coordinator to ensure that quality training is available across the trade groups, and to an annotation system for those Regular air force engineers going from BBMF to other posts to indicate who in future years may replace the protected senior supervisory engineering personnel.

I sense a gross over-run on Richard Winslade's request and will draw matters to a close. Today the Flight faces new challenges in an arena where the survivors of the last great inter-continental struggle have been diminished by time and human frailty to a mere handful, but where public interest for the men and machinery has never been greater, and where demand for the Flight increases year on year. I believe that the changes I have outlined will ensure our ability to sustain our current level of participation for many years to come and I look forward to hearing the tranquillity of English summer afternoons being interrupted by the music of the Merlin and the harsher bark of the Griffon as the Flight continues to display the most beautiful and evocative aircraft ever built.

Sqn Ldr Paul Day OBE, AFC, RAF (Retd)
September 2003

This was originally written as a foreword to the book in 2003 before Paul Day left the Royal Air Force. I have included it and left it unaltered as I feel it gives a very good idea of the position of the Flight today along with its aspirations. The work load and operational procedures are changing to a greater or lesser extent all the time, but this piece gives a good idea of the complexities of running an operation such as the BBMF.

Acknowledgements

It is a formidable task to recall the names of everyone who has helped me with this book over the past twenty years. I will mention all those that my poor old brain can remember, but if I have left anyone out, please forgive me.

First mention must go to the members of the Flight who, without exception, have given freely of their time over the years. Without this generosity nothing would have been achieved. In particular Sqn Ldr C.S.M. 'Scott' Anderson MBE, who was responsible for giving me initial access to the Flight and who supported and encouraged my work at all times. His successors as commanding officers have been Sqn Ldr Tony Banfield, Wg Cdr Chris Booth, Sqn Ldr Colin Patterson, Sqn Ldr Paul Day OBE, AFC, Sqn Ldr Clive Rowley MBE, and Sqn Ldr Al Pinner MBE. All these gentlemen have supported me in my endeavours to photograph the wonderful aeroplanes that make up the Flight.

A special mention must go to Flt Lt Jack Hawkins, the Flight's Adjutant, who is responsible for drawing up the plans for the many appearances made by the Flight each season. He has also drawn the short straw in trying to fit me into the Flight's plans! Without his long-suffering forbearance many pictures in this book would not have been taken.

The bomber and fighter pilots have been very patient, too, waiting for the right weather and light conditions to keep me happy. The late Bill Houldsworth who had actually flown a Lancaster during Operation 'Manna' in Holland in 1945 – and had so many thousand hours on Shackletons that most people had given up counting – was not only a consummate formation pilot in the Lancaster, but also had a wealth of tales to tell. So many hours in Shackletons had left him deaf, so all conversations were carried on at pretty high volume. Lancaster pilots Ed Straw and Stu Reid have also been most generous with their time and effort.

Of the fighter pilots, apart from the 'Major' who's mentioned too many times, the late Merv Payne, Al Martin, John Ward, Paddy O'Flynne, 'Shiney' Simmons, Peter Bouch, Jack Hamill, Al Martin, Jim Wild, Ian Smith and Tim Nolan have all contributed greatly to the photographs for this book.

There are also other members of aircrew who are equally important to the smooth running of the Flight's operations. The navigators Richard Cave (who liaised with the Royal Navy to set up the shot of the Flight overhead HMS *Scylla*), Doug Eke and Tony Down, together with Jeff Hesketh, Dave Chadderton and Andy Marson, have been consistently responsible for getting us all to the right location and on time.

Flight Engineers Nigel Brown, Chuck Knight and Dave Drinkwater have looked after all our airborne mechanical needs; and Air Loadmasters Chris

Massingham and Scott Toomer have kept a beady eye on my safety in the back of the Dakota.

On the ground the unsung heroes of the Flight are the ground crew, who labour to keep the aircraft in pristine condition. When I first worked with the Flight these personnel were very much back room boys. Thanks to the efforts of the then engineering officer, Charles Ness, the situation today is very different with the ground crew getting the recognition they deserve. It was Charles Ness who, after much argument, finally obtained an issue of Nomex flight overalls for those ground crew required to fly in the Lancaster or Devon; due mainly to his argument that 'ground crew burn just as well as aircrew'. The names that come to mind for supplying enthusiasm, lashing tape, electricity etc are Phil Royle, Dave Payne, Pete Downer, Ian Hinks, Barry Sears, Rick Evans, Pete Jeffery (at present with the Flight as a civilian heading the spares recovery programme), Vince Carter, Mike Hall, Paul Wheal, Tim Hudson, Nigel Bunn, Paul Blackah, Norman Pringle, Ian Davies, Jack Dempsey, Keith Brenchley, Dick Harmer, Kevin Martin, Mark Thompson, Clive O'Connell and all the rest, some of whom will no doubt confront me at a later date!

Richard Riding, the founder and long time editor of *Aeroplane Monthly*, has been one of my most enthusiastic supporters over the years. He used many of my images of the Flight in the magazine. My assistants, Andy Henderson and Jonothan Slatter, who put up with many freezing hours hanging about on airfields, together with camera aircraft pilots Ben Kershaw and the late Norman Lees, also deserve a huge vote of thanks. I am also indebted to Rick Allison, who as Commanding Officer of the RAF parachute team, The Falcons, was able to pull the right strings to get me aboard their C-130 Hercules where I was allowed to use the ramp as a camera platform.

Last and by no means least, thanks are due to my editor Jonathan Falconer, and the staff at Sutton Publishing who have shown so much patience during the gestation period of this book.

Richard Winslade
Stroud, March 2007

Author's Introduction

My interest in aviation was kindled at the age of about 12 when I was 'low-levelled' by a Lockheed Ventura close to our house at Blaauwberg Strand near Cape Town in South Africa. I remember soon after this event cycling the 10 miles or so to Ysterplaat airfield to witness the arrival of the Avro Shackletons that were to replace the Ventura in the maritime role and being greatly impressed with the sound of these four-engine machines. I little realised then that I would be part of the farewell flight of this type when they retired from RAF service at Lossiemouth in Scotland some thirty years later, or that the sound of the four Griffons would lose none of its impressiveness over the intervening decades.

I had already made up my mind to pursue a career in photography, having been given an old camera by a friend of the family, who also taught me the basics of developing and printing. It never entered my head to follow a life in aviation, but the interest in aeroplanes aroused in those early years grew and I have been fortunate enough to be able to combine these two passions, giving me the best of both worlds.

I first saw the Battle of Britain Memorial Flight at Old Warden in about 1975 and I remember how depleted the Lancaster looked without its mid-upper turret. (The turret found by Mr J.N. Wortley in Argentina had not yet been fitted.) There were far fewer air displays in those days. Occasional RAF open days at Biggin Hill and Old Warden were the main attractions, with smaller but no less interesting events at locations such as Booker, Popham or Redhill. The displays at Old Warden were eagerly anticipated events and it was here that I managed to develop a technique of ground-to-air photography that could occasionally be mistaken for air-to-air work. At that time my main involvement in photography was in London's advertising industry, producing large format still-life images for advertising and editorial clients. My new-found technique in aviation photography fooled a certain picture editor into believing I was reasonably accomplished at air-to-air work and I was therefore commissioned to illustrate an article about aerobatics by the late Oliver Stewart. This commission introduced me to Neil Williams and 'Manx' Kelly (both sadly no longer with us), who in the short time I knew them taught me so much about flying and were enthusiastic and encouraging about my photography. I flew many photographic sorties with both of them taking pictures of aeroplanes ranging in type from Spitfires to Stampes, Harvards, a Pitts Special and even an Owl Racer!

Looking for a way to finance my involvement with aviation (always remembering that to amass a small fortune in aviation, one needs to start with a large one), I submitted some pictures to Richard Riding at the recently relaunched *Aeroplane Monthly*. He was impressed enough to publish some of these early efforts and over the years was to become a firm friend and 'partner in crime'. It was his use of my work that helped to open many doors for me, one of which led me to the Battle of Britain Memorial Flight, where Sqn Ldr C.S.M. 'Scott' Anderson had recently taken over as Commanding Officer. I had been trying for some time to gain access to the Flight, but an unfortunate clash of personalities between myself and the previous Commanding Officer had proved insurmountable! 'Scott' Anderson had witnessed my efforts and now gave me a chance to prove myself during a transit flight from Manston in Kent to the Flight's home base at RAF Coningsby. Luckily the results were good enough for Richard Riding to use a picture of the Spitfire Mk II and Hurricane PZ865 as a centre-spread. Better still, I managed to carry out the task without delaying the Flight in transit and thus using up their precious allotment of hours, and they also requested copies to hang in the crew-room. Thus began a relationship that has grown over the years to give me unique access to what must be the world's premier vintage aircraft display team.

Over the next five years I amassed a body of work that was published as a book in 1987, giving an in-depth look at all aspects of the Flight. Now, some twenty years later, I have been allowed back to the Flight to update the situation.

Much had changed when I first arrived back at the Flight. Almost all the faces were different – one exception being the pilot of the Spitfire on that first photographic sortie from Manston in 1979, Sqn Ldr Paul Day OBE, AFC. By the time he retired from the Royal Air Force in April 2004, 'The Major' (as he is known to many) had served in the RAF for forty-three years, twenty-four of which were with the BBMF, including nine years as Commanding Officer. During his career with the RAF he served with 14, 20, 28, 54, 63, 64, 65 and 208 Squadrons, and spent time with the 310th, 311th and 550th Tactical Fighter Training Squadrons of the USAF (hence the honorary rank of major). During his career he amassed over 2,000 hours on the Hawker Hunter, 3,000 hours on the Phantom and 1,000 hours on the Tornado. In addition, with the BBMF he accrued over 1,000 hours on the Spitfire alone.

Paul Day's successor was Sqn Ldr Clive Rowley MBE, who had joined the Flight in 1996. He proved to be just as enthusiastic and encouraging as the Major had been, and was happy for me to turn up to take photographs of the Flight at a moment's notice. Clive Rowley took over command in 2003, just as the public profile of the BBMF was being raised higher than ever, with the requests made for appearances at air shows and commemorative events increasing almost by the hour. He brought with him a new awareness of the value of the correct sort of publicity to the Flight, and as well as improving the annual brochure into what now amounts to a collector's item for the enthusiast, he raised the exposure of the Flight throughout the whole spectrum of the media. In 2005, for example, aircraft from the Flight took part in some 320 events and were seen by an estimated six million people. Sqn Ldr Rowley recently completed over 500 hours on the Spitfires and Hurricanes at the Flight, in addition to his impressive total of some 7,000 hours on aircraft as diverse as Bulldogs, Hawks, Lightnings and Tornadoes. He is a joy to photograph in the air as he follows his brief to the letter and is aware of the effects of light and shade, and he thus contributes a great deal to any sortie by placing his aircraft to take advantage of the prevailing conditions.

Clive retired from the RAF at the end of the 2006 display season and his place as Commanding Officer has been taken by Sqn Ldr Al Pinner MBE, who has been a volunteer fighter pilot with the BBMF for the past four years as well as holding down a 'day job' flying Harriers. He has seen action in both the Balkans and Iraq, completing in excess of 100 sorties, and has amassed some 3,800 flying hours during his career. Each Commanding Officer at the BBMF has been a hard act to follow as they have all left their individual marks and improvements on the Flight. It falls to Al Pinner to oversee the celebrations marking the 50th anniversary of the formation of the BBMF, a task that I for one am in no doubt he will take in his stride.

Over the years I have had breaks from working with BBMF, so this book is in no way a chronological account of the fifty years since its formation. Rather, it is a personal view with my favourite photographs of the times I have been privileged to spend with the Flight. There are so many members of the Flight who have helped over the years. Those who have gone, such as Merv Paine and Billy Houldsworth, will unfortunately not see the results of my labours. Thank you *all* for letting me in and giving me such a good time. Thanks also to Reginald Mitchell, Sir Sydney Camm and Roy Chadwick for supplying the raw material!

CHAPTER 1

The Battle of Britain Memorial Flight – A Personal View

My personal involvement with the Battle of Britain Memorial Flight began in 1980. Growing up as I did in the immediate post-Second World War years, I had long been interested in the era of aviation represented by the aircraft operated by the Flight and had for some five years been taking air-to-air photographs of privately owned vintage aeroplanes. In those days the Spitfires and Hurricanes of the BBMF were virtually the only extant airworthy examples of these types. Adrian Swire's Spitfire IX, MH434, was being operated from Booker by Neil Williams and the Shuttleworth Collection's Spitfire Vc had just taken to the air. Doug Arnold also owned a Mk XVI, but this, along with the rest of his collection, was kept under close wraps at Blackbushe. The Flight's Hurricanes were the only examples flying anywhere and the Lancaster, as now, was a rare bird indeed.

My friendship with Neil Williams came about through my being asked to illustrate an article on aerobatics for the *Illustrated London News*, and this led to an introduction to Lt Cdr Chris Johnson, the Commanding Officer of the Royal Navy Historic Flight at RNAS Yeovilton. Neil and I had hit it off from the first meeting and it was his recommend-

ation that gave me access to the Sea Furies, Swordfish and Fireflies operated by this then embryo organisation.

By the late 1970s I had amassed a small portfolio of photographs of their aircraft, together with pictures of other privately owned light aircraft, and it was with these examples of my work that with some trepidation I took the plunge and approached the then Commanding Officer of the BBMF, Sqn Ldr 'Jacko' Jackson. The only other photographers working with the BBMF at that time were Arthur Gibson and Richard Wilson, both of whom were well established with a track record to match.

My trepidation was well founded. From the off Sqn Ldr Jackson did not take to me. It was probably the fact that I came from the flamboyant world of advertising in London that put him off! I persevered, however, and after a year of turning up at various locations with a hired camera aeroplane only to be told that for one reason or another it was all too difficult, I was finally given three minutes in formation with Hurricane LF363 over Bournemouth. With its many caravan sites and associated holiday locations is hardly the best backdrop for air-to-air photography, but a few frames were usable. So, having printed and framed the best two or three, I

The start of it all. Neil Williams flies the Shuttleworth Spitfire V in its first public display at Old Warden. The combination of the close proximity of the display axis to the crowd (giving a large crisp image on a medium length lens) and a day of dark clouds with strong light at a low angle beneath helps give the impression that the aircraft is actually flying above cloud.

Opposite: Neil Williams loops a Stampe at the Tiger Club at Redhill in Surrey. The camera aircraft, also a Stampe, was being flown by his wife Lynn. Neil Williams was British Aerobatics Champion twelve times. He was enthusiastic and encouraging about my photography and did a great deal to further my early ambitions in the world of aviation. Both Neil and his wife were killed in 1977 when the Spanish Heinkel 111 they were ferrying to England crashed in the Pyrenees.

again contacted the Flight to arrange delivery. Upon my arrival I discovered that Sqn Ldr Jackson had retired, his place being taken by Sqn Ldr C.S.M. 'Scott' Anderson. We spoke briefly and I handed over the prints, little realising that this change of command at the Flight was about to give me a chance to prove myself and ultimately gain access to the Flight – not to mention forging a friendship that has lasted to this day. I must say at this point that I have met 'Jacko' Jackson on a couple of occasions since and have found him to be a most affable and helpful man.

At the time of my fruitless attempts to carry out air-to-air photography with the Flight, 'Scott' Anderson had been in his probationary period as the new Commanding Officer of the Flight. Unknown to me, he had taken note of my tenacity and had resolved to give me a chance to show what I could do! I was delighted to receive his telephone call inviting me up to RAF Coningsby to discuss what I wanted to do and how best to achieve my aims.

I remember well the first proper sortie I carried out with the Flight. At a face-to-face briefing with all concerned, it was arranged that we would meet over

Headcorn, from where I had hired a twin-engine Partenavia aircraft. The Flight was to make a transit flight from Manston in Kent, where they had landed to refuel, to their base at RAF Coningsby. Now I was to learn at first hand the meaning of the oft-used phrase in vintage aviation, 'If you've time to spare, travel by air!'

Vintage aircraft are, if they are to be flown safely, only operated when weather conditions fall within very strict limits. Needless to say, on the chosen date and for the next two days the weather conditions were out of limits for the Flight's aircraft to operate. So my assistant and I ensconced ourselves in a local hostelry at Headcorn and kept in touch with both our pilot and the members of the Flight at Manston. At last the weather cleared and gave us one of those days that air-to-air photographers pray for: light wind conditions and fluffy cumulus at about 2,000 feet.

We were airborne a good half an hour before the allotted time and loitered at about 3,000 feet above Headcorn, all the while keeping a sharp look out for the Lancaster, Spitfire and Hurricane. Right at the arranged time the Flight emerged through the clouds. It was a sight that will remain with me for the rest of my life. The photographs we had arranged to take were what I describe as portrait shots – that is, simple formation flying with pleasing backgrounds to produce good crisp images of each aircraft. One image from this session remains in my opinion one of the best aeroplane pictures I have ever taken. The sunlight on the aeroplanes, together with the perfect English summer background, is powerfully evocative of that hot summer of 1940. It is also close to the quality obtained by Charles E. Brown in some of his work. To my mind, Charles is the best air-to-air photographer of all time. His awareness of the environment in which he placed his subjects gave his pictures a feeling of flying that few have achieved either before or since.

At last, after much perseverance, I had managed to carry out some air-to-air photography with the Flight. I mounted and framed the prints and took them up to Coningsby. Everyone was impressed and Scott suggested that he might use one in the next brochure produced for the Flight. (Scott was largely responsible for improving the annual brochure from the single-page affair it was when he arrived at the Flight to ten far glossier pages. It has since been further expanded and improved by successive Commanding Officers to become the sought-after and informative forty-odd pages it is today.) Scott also wanted some photographs of the Spitfire V AB910 for the same brochure and so we arranged an air meet above RAF Wattisham as the fighters made a transit from home base to Biggin Hill.

The Rothmans Aerobatic Team over the Chilterns near their home at Booker in 1976.

Opposite: Manx Kelly knife-edges his Pitts S2a for the camera. This photograph was used on the front cover of the *Illustrated London News* as a link with the article about aerobatics by Oliver Stewart. Manx was the founder of the Rothmans Aerobatic Team which was based at Booker, initially using Stampe aircraft but later transferring to the Curtis Pitts S2a. He was killed in America in a Stolpe Acroduster when the top wing detached itself from the aircraft while it was being flown inverted at low level.

Now I have known Sqn Ldr Paul Day for many years and I am sure that anything I say about Wattisham he will emphatically deny! From memory, I think this was Paul's first year with the Flight, and it was certainly the first time he had been allowed to lead the fighter formation. Now, charging about in Phantoms or similar heavy metal, covering vast tracts of ground in very little time, is very different from map-reading a vintage fighter above the countryside on a summer's afternoon. A pilot of huge experience, with thousands of hours in many types of aircraft, he became what he described as

Lt Cdr Peter Shepherd (left) with Lt Cdr Chris Johnson standing in front of the Royal Navy Historic Flight's Hawker Sea Fury at RNAS Yeovilton. Lt Cdr Johnson was instrumental in helping me reach many goals in aviation photography. Peter Shepherd's displays in the Sea Fury were immaculate and particularly impressive at Old Warden, where the crowd always waited for the sound of the aircraft's slipstream following the high-speed pass between the trees to the north of the airfield.

'Ho Hum' about the relativity of time passed and distance covered, and positively identified Honington as Wattisham. He made one orbit of the airfield and, as we were nowhere to be seen, continued on – only to then pass over Wattisham where he realised his mistake! By this point there was insufficient time left for the air-to-air slot, which had to be abandoned. It speaks volumes for the man that the next day he telephoned me to apologise and explain. We all learned lessons from this. I have never again arranged to carry out a sortie other than from the same airfield as the subject aircraft, and I know that whenever Paul gets at all uppity with me I need only mention Wattisham to shut him up!

Make no mistake, Paul is a fine pilot with thousands of hours' experience in fast jets and well over a thousand hours' experience in Spitfires and Hurricanes, making him the most experienced 'warbird' pilot in the world. He has all the arrogance, albeit often tongue-in-cheek, of the fast jet driver. He is also the first to admit his short-comings and failures (if indeed there are any). He has been instrumental in enabling me to follow my dream of photographing these wonderful examples of our aviation heritage. He is also the most wonderful raconteur, and I shall try here to recount his first meeting with a piston-engined tail-wheel aircraft, which took the form of the humble De

Havilland Chipmunk. He told this story one evening and had us all in stitches.

Paul Day was one of the first intake into the RAF who learned to fly on jets from the outset. He progressed from the Jet Provost to the Hunter and on to the F4 Phantom. He had joined the Royal Air Force to fly and when it came to the choice of promotion or flying, he opted for the Specialist Aircrew route which enabled him to keep flying rather than going for promotion and perhaps a desk job. An experienced pilot, he thought he could handle almost anything the Air Force could throw at him.

So when he volunteered for the Battle of Britain Memorial Flight the thought of flying the little Chipmunk held no fears at all. (The Flight uses two Chipmunks as initial trainers and also to keep pilots current on piston-engined tail-wheel aircraft.) The Chipmunk, however, is a completely different kettle of fish from what Paul was used to. Compared with a Phantom it weighs nothing, and thus is at the mercy of every breath of wind and turbulence, and landing requires techniques completely alien to a fast jet driver. By his own admission the take-off was

more than adequate and the ensuing flying and simple manoeuvres equally so. However, by his sixth attempt at landing a small crowd had gathered on the balcony of the control tower to watch the fun. After another couple of attempts his instructor did the honours, got out without a word and left Paul to think about it! He has progressed more than

One of the first sorties I carried out with the Royal Navy Historic Flight was with their Swordfish on the way to the Bath & West Show. The camera aircraft on that occasion was the Historic Flight's faithful Chipmunk.

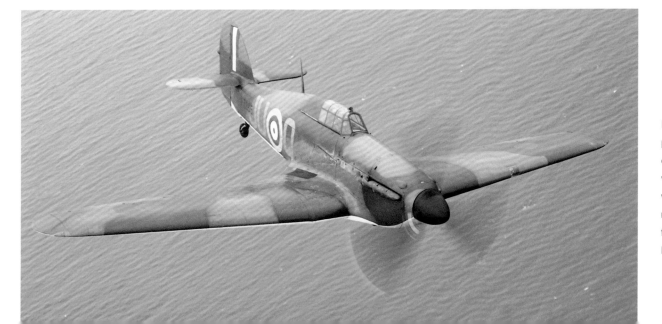

My first attempt at air-to-air photography with the Battle of Britain Memorial Flight was out of Bournemouth, when I was given three minutes to get what I could from the open door of a Piper Seneca.

A great deal more successful was my next attempt when the Flight was transiting home to Coningsby from Manston in Kent. We were blessed with one of those beautiful late summer days with broken cumulus at about 2,000 feet. This shot against the clouds, of P7350 piloted by Sqn Ldr Paul Day, remains one of my all-time favourites.

Opposite: An Avro Shackleton AEW2 of 8 Squadron flies over RAF Lossiemouth for the last time. Piloted by Wg Cdr Chris Booth, the Commanding Officer of the squadron, she was off to visit the many places in the British Isles that had connections with this long-serving aircraft, before being auctioned off along with her two remaining sisters. The Flight used the Shackletons of 8 Squadron to train the Lancaster's crews.

somewhat on tail-draggers since those days! When he retired from the Air Force at the beginning of 2004, he did so as the longest serving member of the BBMF flight crew and also its longest serving Commanding Officer.

But back to the plot. I had long been impressed by the almost head-on angles that photographers like Charles E. Brown and Charles Simms had been able to achieve. I knew that these pictures in many cases were taken from the rear turret of a Lancaster (in the days when there were many of this type in the air,

making such a platform easy to organise), or in the case of the photography taken for the annual Farnborough display from the open back of a Fairchild Packet. The latter being unavailable, I began to pester Scott Anderson for the opportunity to use the rear turret of PA474 to photograph the fighters. To keep me quiet, and I suspect to give himself an easier life, Scott sought permission to carry me on transit flights. I think it was no small surprise to both of us when this permission was granted.

The rear turret of the Lancaster provides an admirable platform, not least because it boasts a clear vision aperture by means of a sliding section in the Perspex. Clear vision is almost essential, as however clean a Perspex canopy may be, there is always the danger of distortion and also of reflections ruining what might otherwise be perfect images. In addition, the exhaust trails from the Merlins curve outboard, thus giving no problem with heat haze distortion, and the Lancaster has sufficient speed to allow the fighters more freedom of movement than they have when working with an aircraft that has imposed limits once doors or hatches have been removed. The rear ramp of a Hercules, for example, might seem ideal for photography but in fact the exhaust trails curve inwards and slightly down, converging into a grey 'blob' that prohibits anything other than a 2 degree downward angle for the subject aircraft.

My first trip in the rear turret of the Lancaster was a short 'out and home' to a fly-past at Norwich, which allowed me to work with the fighters for ten minutes on each leg. Luckily, it proved the point I had been trying to make and it was established that as long as I could prove it necessary, and it was either on a transit flight or a fly-past, I was welcome to use the rear turret for photography.

Working from this position in the Lancaster is cramped and has its problems. I am not the smallest person in the world (and I now understand why rear gunners were in general not six-footers) and squeezing between the gun mountings to get my head and camera out of the clear vision panel required a certain amount of contortion on my part. All directions to the subject aircraft are given by hand signals, but I still had to wear a helmet with headphones and a face mask microphone to remain in contact with the pilot of the Lancaster, and we learned early on that I would need to change to using a throat-mike with an on/off switch taped to the camera as it was all too easy to knock the mike switch on the face mask to the 'on' position. This meant that all the ambient sound from me, the slipstream and the general hiss from the communications system drowned out all communications between other members of the crew.

Once I was 'wedged' out of my clear vision hatch it was no easy matter to reach the switch on my face mask to turn it off, and the interference caused by it being on didn't appear to register in my headphones. The change to a throat-mike came about after I became aware, through my headphones, of the voice of Scott Anderson saying 'Will someone get down the back with an axe and cut that ******* off'. I thought I had blown it for good but the long-suffering Scott, realising the problem, gave me another chance.

It wasn't until recently, while reading Charles Simms's book *Camera in the Sky*, that I realised the dangers associated with working from the rear turret of the Lancaster, and how wise I had been never to

CPO Ron Gourlay in the back of the Swordfish over Normandy during the rehearsal for the 40th anniversary celebrations of the D-Day landings in 1944. Despite the vastly disparate speeds, it was contrived that the Lancaster and the Swordfish would appear 'in formation', albeit briefly, when they over flew the saluting base at Arromanches.

totally remove my harness – I only loosened it enough to give me access to my window on the world. It appears that under certain conditions a vacuum can be formed behind the rear turret, leading to a situation where there is little or no resistance to gradually falling out. This nearly happened to Simms while he was photographing a Hawker Hunter, and it was only the quick wit of his assistant, sitting on the catwalk leading to the turret, that saved him. Realising the situation, he grabbed Simms's legs just in time to stop him going into free-fall.

I may have been slightly disparaging about the Hercules. The ramp is a great platform, but it does have more restrictions than the Lancaster. The best aspect of working off the ramp of a Hercules is the feeling of being alone combined with the feeling of power. Obviously you are attached to the airframe by a sturdy harness but once on the edge of the ramp you cannot see even peripherally anything of the

Three Merlins in formation: Paul Day cruises off the Lancaster's wing during the crossing to the Channel Islands.

Flight Engineer Nigel Brown at his station in the Lancaster. This image was taken in the days before hard hats became a sensible requirement for the Flight's aircrew.

airframe unless you look directly downwards. This gives the impression of travelling through the air backwards completely unaided! The feeling of power comes when the formation is joined and the photography begins. As described earlier, all instructions to other aircraft are given by hand signals and it is quite amazing to see a Spitfire or Lancaster in close line-astern formation responding to my every

indicated request. It feels like I should be wearing tails and waving a baton in front of an orchestra at the Albert Hall!

Of the other aircraft I have used as a camera platform the North American Harvard must rate among the best. It is roomy and has a great field of vision, and has a speed range that is acceptable to most vintage aircraft types. At the lower end of the speed range however, when a high power setting is required to keep the aeroplane in the air, a high-frequency vibration is set up that leads to camera shake and thus un-sharp pictures. This could be overcome by using a faster shutter speed but this would 'freeze' the propeller of the subject aircraft giving the impression of engine failure. Unfortunately the Harvard has become an expensive beast to operate in this country and general use for air-to-air work has thus declined.

The Yak 52 has to a great extent become a replacement for the Harvard for general air-to-air work. It is cheaper to operate, gives the option of shooting out of either side of the cockpit and has a reasonable speed range. Other mounts I have used include the Piper Lance, which can be flown with the rear passenger door removed. The restricted speed designated for this set-up is 150mph, which is enough to give some range of manoeuvrability to most piston-engined fighters. The Lance also has a high tail-plane (a T-tail) so one has a clear view aft. This is the only clear vision view obtainable from this aircraft, and so all pictures will have the subject travelling from left to right. Similarly, the De Havilland Chipmunk has a clear vision facility through the removable escape hatch in the rear cockpit, making it an ideal platform for the photography of lighter types.

Air-to-air photography requires the aircraft to fly in close formation and therefore you have to be confident in the respective pilots' capabilities. In the early years of my doing this sort of work I was given

Flt Lt Richard 'Dickie Mint'
Cave at the navigator's table
in the Lancaster cockpit.

a couple of frights by people who claimed to have current formation experience – only to find subsequently that their definition of 'current' was 'within the past few years'! It is imperative that a thorough briefing is carried out. It is pointless getting airborne and just stooging about, hoping that something will eventually fall into place. You must have a clear idea of what you want the final image to look like and you must stick to the briefed plan to achieve this end. This is not to say that there are not happy accidents of positioning and light that give unplanned images which can often be better than those originally briefed. But the costs involved in getting airborne with a camera ship and subject aircraft dictate that one has to end up with a usable result.

Air-to-air photography is obviously the 'glamorous' side of the business, but there is much more to the Flight than turning up at designated air shows. The enthusiasm and meticulous planning on the part of the aircrew to achieve the goals of some 500 appearances by various aircraft of the Flight, together with the love and devotion lavished on the airframes by the ground crew are to my mind almost more interesting than the actual flying. The Flight is very much a family and the trust between aircrew and ground crew is total. Then too, there are the private specialists who in their own way will move heaven and earth to keep the Flight in the air. Retro Track and Air, Vintage Fabrics and the Aircraft Restoration Company are cases in point.

Rolls-Royce Merlin and Griffon maintenance is carried out by Retro Track and Air at Cam in Gloucestershire. This company has created an enviable reputation over the past few years as experts in the restoration and overhaul of aero engines in general and the Merlin in particular. They are the first choice of a great many Merlin-powered 'warbird' owners and are the MOD-preferred rebuilder of all Merlin and Griffon engines for the BBMF. This is due to their close working relationship with the Flight. The Flight's aircraft can put in as many as 100 hours per aircraft per annum, and drawing on their experience of operating the Merlin and Griffon engines, the Flight and Retro have joined forces to instigate some eleven modifications to the manufacturer's specifications that ensure even more reliability and longevity from an already tried and trusted power unit. They have concentrated on the 'top end' of the engine, the area that is known to be one of the weaker areas of the power plant, and have facilities for regrinding and polishing camshafts to the very highest standards. The workmanship is more akin to precision watch-making than to power plant engineering!

Such high standards are neither easy nor cheap to achieve: it takes around 2,000 man-hours to strip and rebuild an engine. There are approximately 10,500 parts in a Merlin or Griffon engine, including nuts and bolts, but even if you halve that number, and then take into account that 80 per cent of the resulting number of parts have to be individually tested, it gives some idea of where the time and the money are used up. But at 500ft and 400mph the quality of the work is remembered long after the cost has been forgotten.

In reassembling the engine, particular attention is paid to the camshaft and rocker assembly, this being the Achilles heel of both the Merlin and Griffon engines. These parts are particularly rigidly inspected and tested, hard chromed and reground to the

unique profile that gives the engines their characteristic growl.

Retro Track and Air is based on the edge of a quiet Cotswold village and it would do little for relations with the local residents were they to operate the fruits of their labours at plus 18psi and 3,000rpm on site. Their unique solution to this problem is a flat-bed Dodge truck which has been converted into a mobile test rig with interchangeable engine mounts to house either a Merlin or a Griffon engine. Once the engine has been installed, the rig is driven to nearby Kemble airfield where ground-running is carried out and monitored through the on-board dynamometer to measure torque and power output.

The meticulous work carried out by this firm led the then Commanding Officer of the BBMF, Sqn Ldr Paul Day, to describe the Flight's introduction to Retro Track and Air as 'serendipitous'. It is true that they play a large part in keeping the aircraft flying, so that your Sunday afternoon snooze can suddenly be interrupted by the distant growl of a Merlin or Griffon as a fighter transits between displays.

Although the engineering section at the Flight has the expertise to undertake deep servicing and rebuilds of airframes, the pressing commitments of the small force of engineers dictates that this time-consuming work must be sent out to civilian specialist firms. One such organisation is the Aircraft Restoration Company based at the Imperial War Museum airfield at Duxford in Cambridgeshire. John Romaine, the head of this organisation, has been involved in aircraft engineering and flying since his youth and as a member of Graham Warner's team was involved in the immaculate restoration of the world's only airworthy Bristol Blenheim. He is also a more than competent display pilot and knows only too well the high standards required not only to restore the airframes to perfect original condition, but also to ensure that safety is never compromised.

Another key person in this group of skilled 'outsiders' is Clive Denney, the wizard with Irish linen. He is one of a rapidly diminishing number of craftsmen who have the skill to cover airframes with fabric and dope. As the control surfaces on all the fighters are fabric-covered he is regularly employed by the Flight to undertake running repairs and to complete the fabric sections on any rebuilding work. He is the master of the spray-gun and the paint brush and his paint finishes on vintage aircraft are superb. As a result he is in great demand and his specialist firm Vintage Fabrics, based in Essex, is as a matter of course overloaded with work from the vintage aircraft community. Denney too has graduated to flying Spitfires and pilots' privately owned machines at many air shows during the summer season. In 2006 he resprayed AB910 in the desert camouflage and markings of Wg Cdr Richard Gleed and hand-painted Gleed's personal emblem of 'Figaro the Cat' on the fuselage.

To be able to watch these specialists working and photograph in detail what they achieve and how they do it is truly fascinating. I tend to become obsessed with that with which they have become obsessed, while at the same time seeing it all from a totally different angle. It is a privilege to be able to

Forty years of fighter evolution in close formation: Sqn Ldr Paul Day and Wg Cdr Rick Peacock-Edwards formate on the rear turret of the Lancaster to give the impression of some weird hybrid machine. This photograph was taken during the transit to Abingdon in 1985, where the two aircraft were to give their last display as a pair.

watch Stuart Watts put bits of an engine together or to watch Clive Denney respraying an airframe, using the identical techniques, albeit on a far larger scale, to those used by those among us who make detailed scale models of these aeroplanes.

The techniques I use for the engineering and ground photography are those learned from many years as a commercial photographer. The pictures have to be 'set up' to achieve the desired effects and I find that the best way of doing this is to make a visit in advance of the actual shoot to work out what exactly is needed on the day. If both I and the subject have a good idea of what to expect, it takes a great deal less time and creates a lot less disruption to the tight schedules that these people work to. The equipment too is simple – a camera with wide angle, standard and medium length lenses, and inter-changeable film magazines (including a Polaroid back as insurance!). Light is provided, if needed, by two old but trusty Bowens 850 flash units with various diffusers and reflectors, etc., together with miles of gaffer tape.

My time spent photographing the BBMF has been punctuated by taking part in some memorable events both in this country and on the continent. One of these was the rehearsal for the 40th anniversary of the D-Day landings in Normandy, and another the celebrations marking the 40th anniversary of Operation Manna, when the Allies dropped supplies at the end of the war to the population of Holland, who had been left in a state of starvation by the retreating German army.

This latter event involved the Lancaster along with a Spitfire and Hurricane from the Flight making a transit to Gilze Rijen in Holland to take part in a massed fly-past by aircraft from the RAF and USAF. In those days the Flight didn't have the luxury of a support aircraft, and as the ground crew and all their tools had to be ferried across to Holland in the Lancaster, my assistant Andy

Henderson and I had to take the ferry from Norwich to the Hook of Holland and make our own way to Gilze Rijen. Once there, however, we were assured of a place on the Lancaster to record the main event.

The Dutch are the most hospitable people I have ever had the privilege to meet. From the outset they adopted the premise that our money was no good. Their hospitality was almost embarrassing: we were not allowed to pay for anything. Absolutely everything was supplied for us, from fuel for the aircraft to food and accommodation for all of us. In vain I tried to explain that I was only a 'hanger-on' and that I should be allowed at least to contribute. In the end it was arranged that on the day after the main fly-past, when the Lancaster was due to make a leaflet drop over the coast, I would be furnished with a ride in a Harvard to obtain air-to-air photographs of this event. (I should explain here that the Dutch Harvard club is situated on the airfield at Gilze Rijen and the club's members had been tasked with hosting us for the duration of our visit.)

The main fly-past was carried out as planned but ended up less spectacular than had been hoped, due mainly to the USAF's insistence that there be at least 2 miles separation between the various formations. As some of the ground crew had been taken off to view the event from a VIP position in Amsterdam, we were very light on crew for the Lancaster and I found myself detailed to be in charge of the token drop of sweets as we passed over Falkenberg on our way home. These days this sort of event would be organised to the nth degree, with the parachute and package being released electrically from the bomb bay of the Lancaster. But in 1985, these things were done in a different and in some ways more charming manner.

The tin of sweets had been attached to a small drogue parachute and I was to push this contraption out of the clear vision panel in the rear turret of the

bomber. I positioned myself for the run-in to Falkenberg and awaited the countdown and release order from Scott. When the order came I bundled the lot out but the lines to the parachute were rather too long and the whole thing was pulled out at great speed, nearly taking me with it. I believe the sweets were well received by the assembled children, despite the fact that the parachute was rather inadequate for the weight of the tin, which landed hard and burst upon impact, scattering sweets in all directions.

During the fly-past and parachute drop the weather had been gradually deteriorating and by the time we got back to Gilze Rijen it was only just good enough for the Lancaster to go off on the leaflet raid. The leaflets (facsimiles of the last issue of the Dutch wartime underground newspaper *Die Vliegende Hollander* – The Flying Dutchman) were loaded into the bomb bay and six more bundles went into the rear cockpit of the Harvard: once again, by default, I was to be in charge of a commemorative drop on Dutch soil.

We took off in fast-fading late afternoon light and by the time we reached the coast we had lost contact with the Lancaster – flying in and out of low cloud,

The Flight turns towards Sark for a final low pass before heading home. Cpl Pete 'Gerbs' Jeffery in the mid-upper turret obviously has designs on the Major in P7350!

As LF363 taxies in from her display, the grand finale of the display at Middle Wallop begins. Reminiscent of a scene from the film *Apocalypse Now*, some fifty Army Air Corps helicopters rise from behind the trees on the far side of the airfield to carry out a 'march-past' and salute.

we deemed it safer to keep our distance. We finally caught a glimpse of her in the gloom as she made her drop and then we prepared to run in ourselves. The bundles of leaflets in the Harvard had been tied with string and I had armed myself with a Swiss Army knife to deal with this before heaving the bundles out of our aircraft. Unfortunately for me, someone at the airfield, trying to be helpful, had already cut the string on two of the bundles, with the result that as soon as I slid the cockpit canopy forward I was engulfed in a snowstorm of flying paper. Fortunately the pilot's canopy was closed and none of the leaflets was sucked into the forward cockpit. Indeed, the pilot was completely unaware of the mayhem that was taking place just behind him! By this time the weather had deteriorated further and we had to divert to Schiphol and required a QDM from their Air Traffic Controllers in order to find our way. We landed without incident to find the whole empennage of our machine draped with the remains of our leaflets.

We returned to Gilze Rijen the following morning and spent the day visiting various places of interest, including Guy Gibson's grave. As Gilze Rijen is the main wreckage recovery and investigation centre for the Dutch Air Force we were also given a guided tour of this department, which was sometimes involved in recovering wartime wrecks from the Zuider Zee. That evening a party had been arranged at a local hotel, and it turned into a truly memorable night. The food was absolutely superb and a BBMF crest about 3 feet across had been made out of seafood as a centrepiece. The hotel was large and there was a wedding reception taking place in one of the other function rooms. Once the bride and groom discovered who we were, we were all duly invited, and what a night it was! I often wonder what happened to that couple. They were barely old enough to remember the war, but they opened their lives to us that night and made us very welcome.

Earlier that same year the Flight had taken part in the fly-past to commemorate the D-Day landings in

Normandy. I had been able to wangle my way on to the Lancaster for one of the rehearsals and on to the Royal Navy Historic Flight Swordfish for the second. I was not able to secure a place on the actual day, though, as the BBC quite rightly had been given the first option on this privilege. The brief for this particular operation was that the Lancaster, in formation with the Swordfish, would pass over the saluting base at Arromanches just before the Queen gave her address. The person responsible for this obviously had no idea of the problems this would cause, given that the top speed of the Swordfish is almost the stalling speed of the Lancaster.

For this sortie we based ourselves initially on Jersey in the Channel Islands, from where we made the transit to Cherbourg to meet the Swordfish and work out some way of achieving what we had been detailed to do. At Cherbourg we found that President Reagan of the USA had arrived and we were plagued by security checks at every move throughout our stay. Sqn Ldr Scott Anderson and

Lt Cdr Ken Patrick duly met and worked out a plan. The Swordfish would lead off some 2 miles ahead of the Lancaster and at 5 miles from the saluting base it would contact the Lancaster, enabling it to overtake at precisely the time the two aircraft passed over the assembled dignitaries. The main problem was that French Air Traffic Control, which was having to direct the many different aircraft involved in the fly-past, had imposed radio silence for the duration of the run-in and the actual fly-past. The problem was solved by CPO Ron Gourlay, who reckoned, and was proved correct, that it could all be achieved with the use of a good old-fashioned Aldis lamp and Morse code!

After two rehearsals the timing was spot on and the fly-past went perfectly. The original brief on

Ensconced in the back seat on the way to an air-to-air shoot.

Opposite: Built in 1949, De Havilland Devon VP981 went to the Flight from service at Northolt. She served with the Flight from 1985 until 1993, when she was replaced by the Dakota. One of the most comfortable aircraft to fly in, the Devon must also be one of the most aesthetically pleasing commercial aeroplanes ever built.

what to do after the event was that all aircraft should turn inland and return to Cherbourg. On the day, however, Air Traffic insisted, despite query, that the Lancaster turn on to a reciprocal course, thus taking it over the saluting base for a second time. The bomber duly arrived at low level just in time to drown out the beginning of the Queen's address! Despite explanations, blame from on high was apportioned to the navigator on the Lancaster, who was banished to a practice range in Wales for a good number of years. Still, it was here that he met his future wife, and Mr and Mrs Eke now live in Tattershall, not a million miles away from RAF Coningsby, where until recently they ran the refreshment side of the visitors' centre at the Flight.

Another photographic sortie was to record the display formation of a Spitfire PR XIX and a Tornado F2. This was the brainchild of the then AOC 11 Group, the late Ken Hayr, and the then Fighter Leader of the BBMF, Paul Day. This pair put on a very impressive but rather noisy display routine during the 1985 season. The noisy bit was the Tornado, flown by Wg Cdr Richard Peacock-Edwards, carrying out tight turns on full reheat while endeavouring to keep within the confines of the airfield. In the Spitfire Paul Day had an easier task with his lighter and more manoeuvrable machine.

When it came to carrying out the air-to-air photography of the duo, it was the Lancaster's task to go as fast as permitted, while the Tornado was reduced to hanging everything out apart from the undercarriage in an effort to reduce speed enough to hold formation. We carried out a dress rehearsal during a short trip to a fly-past at Louth, with a view to carrying out the shoot itself on the transit to the annual display at RAF Abingdon the following week.

As usual, come the day, the weather was not the best and we had to grab what we could under an overcast sky, but the results were fine and produced some unique images. The main brief was to shoot the formation head-on from the rear turret of the Lancaster but there was also a requirement to supply a shot of both aircraft off the wing of the Lancaster over Abingdon for the *Royal Air Force News*. We had picked specific areas of countryside over the route of the transit to give the best looking backdrop, the last of which was an area of Oxfordshire about 20 miles from Abingdon, thus giving me only a short time to get from the rear turret to the cockpit. This may seem a small point but it was no easy matter, requiring endurance and agility. First I had to unplug my intercom cable, undo my safety harness and then feel behind my back for the catch to open the sliding doors of the turret. With the doors open, I wriggled backwards on my behind on to the catwalk leading one over the spar of the tail-plane, all the while hanging on to the camera for dear life. Having dismounted via the top of the Elsan, I entered the main body of the aircraft. Apart from the danger of braining myelf on the structure of the mid-upper turret (at this time there was no requirement to wear hard hats in the bomber, so Mk 1 cloth inners were the usual headgear), the journey now became easier for a short while. Once on to the top of the bomb bay I came to the really difficult bit: the main spar! This structure is just too high and too wide to clamber over either easily or elegantly, and I ended up in a heap next to the flight engineer, rather bruised but still clutching my camera. When I was plugged once again into the intercom there was a remark from the Boss asking what had taken me so long! Anyway, I was in position just as we began our run-in over Abingdon and got the shot that was needed.

This incident was rather amusing, but I am the first to admit that being in the Lancaster at all is a privilege and the experience will be with me for ever. It does, however, make you wonder what the hell it must have been like for a frightened young man to have to make that short journey in the dark in an

aircraft that was damaged or on fire. It doesn't really bear thinking about.

Photography with the Flight has become more difficult in some ways over the years. Given the increased number of displays they now put on each year and the lack of commensurate increase in the hours allotted to the aircraft, there is little air time spare to be dedicated to photography. The ruling that no passengers apart from essential ground crew can be carried in the bomber during a display may be completely logical but it is frustrating in that many great opportunities during transits to and from displays where the bomber is not scheduled to land are lost to photographers such as me. It has, however, produced a new breed of photographers among the ground crew. Keith Brenchley is one such and he produces some quite stunning work, a fact that doesn't make me envy him any the less!

The professionalism in the Flight has remained at a consistently high level throughout my association with it, and I mean in no way to be derogatory to those who went before when I say that in recent years it has had to become a 'tighter ship'. It never has been the exclusive flying club that some, obviously jealous, individuals have referred to. It has always been a serious professional operation. However, changes in the Royal Air Force mean that there is no longer a pool of pilots or engineers to draw on who have experience of piston engines. With the demise of the Shackleton, pilots with supercharged multi-engine experience soon became a thing of the past, so there is no easy transition to the Flight. The change from current service aircraft to the aircraft operated by the Flight requires extra application from the aircrews, and hand in hand with that goes a more serious attitude towards the job. The knowledge that they are in charge of an irreplaceable part of the country's heritage leads to a sense of responsibility that hasn't altered over the years, but today the step up to the Flight doesn't happen as easily as it may have done in the past.

The fact that things no longer happen as easily or for that matter as cheaply as formerly has dictated that the Flight now has to maintain a far higher profile than it did even five years ago. It has to be seen to be 'paying its way' with appearances each season at an ever-increasing number of displays and national events. To this end Sqn Ldr Clive Rowley was the ideal Commanding Officer. As well as being a careful and consummate pilot and team leader, he was very aware of the importance of exposure for the Flight in both the aviation press and the national media. At this point, with all the talk of cutbacks and frequent rumours of the disbandment of both the Red Arrows and the BBMF because of running costs, both need to maintain a high profile to ensure their continued existence. The engineering costs continue to spiral upwards each year. Because of a shortage of man hours, the Flight is increasingly reliant on outside companies to fulfill their engineering needs. This is not to say that the ground crews at the Flight are not capable of an in-depth overhaul of the Lancaster, because they are, but with all their other daily duties on the Flight there are simply not enough hours in the year to achieve this and keep the Flight operational.

A great deal of teamwork and support is needed to keep these remarkable machines in the air. The ethic of hard work has been a constant factor throughout my association with the Flight. The other constant has been the unpredictable British weather and the engineering unpredictability of operating these very special aeroplanes. I have often thought that if I had a penny for every hour I had spent on the ground waiting to get airborne to carry out air-to-air photography of the Flight I would be a rich man.

CHAPTER 2

A Brief History of the Flight

On 15 September 1945 hundreds of RAF fighters took part in a fly-past over London to commemorate Britain's 'Finest Hour' and to celebrate the return to peace after six years of war.

It was fitting that this and subsequent annual fly-pasts should be led by a Spitfire and a Hurricane, but by the mid-1950s only one Hurricane (LF363) remained in airworthy condition with the RAF and Spitfires too had been phased out of service. By June 1957 even the three civilian-operated Spitfire XIXs (PM631, PS853 and PS915) of the Temperature and Humidity Monitoring Flight at Woodvale had carried out their last sortie. Upon their retirement they were handed back to the RAF and were flown by their civilian pilots to Duxford. From there, accompanied by three Hawker Hunters and three Gloster Javelins, they were ferried by three veteran pilots, Gp Capt 'Johnny' Johnson, Gp Capt James Rankin and Wg Cdr Peter Thompson, to Biggin Hill, where they joined the sole Hurricane to form what was to be known as the Historic Aircraft Flight.

In September of that year PS915 was taken to West Malling, where she was to remain, after a painstaking rebuild by British Aerospace at Samlesbury, until her eventual return to the Battle of Britain Memorial Flight in 1986. Later that year two Spitfire XVIs (TE476 and SL574), which had been used as static exhibits at the Royal Tournament, were also handed over to RAF Biggin Hill, where they were restored to airworthy condition and joined the other aircraft at the Flight.

The Flight's stay at Biggin Hill was to be short-lived as the RAF closed it as an operational station in 1958 and the Flight moved on to North Weald. This was to prove an even more temporary home and in May that year the Flight found itself at Martlesham Heath in a slightly depleted condition as another Spitfire XIX (PS853) was allocated to West Raynham to act as gate guardian. Fortunately she was kept in airworthy condition and was able to rejoin the Flight in 1964.

In 1959 one of the Spitfire XVIs (SL574) suffered an engine failure over London during the annual fly-past and had to carry out a forced landing on the OXO cricket pitch at Bromley in Kent. It was decided after this incident that the risk of operating the Spitfires and Hurricane over London was too great and subsequently they no longer led the annual fly-past. SL574 was rebuilt as a static airframe and for many years was gate guardian at Bentley Priory. There was also at that time some unsubstantiated reasoning that the American-built Packard Merlin was an unreliable engine and therefore the other

PA474 pictured after her conversion to PR1 configuration ahead of delivery to 82 Squadron. *(Aeroplane Monthly Archive)*

Mk XVI was grounded and given to RAF Northolt as a gate guardian. Subsequently in 1986 SL547 was rebuilt at Halton and since 1992 has been on display at the San Diego Aerospace Museum in the guise of N3310; TE476 was recovered in 1989 by Historic Flying Ltd from its post at Northolt and after a rebuild to airworthy status has also crossed the Atlantic to a new home with Kermit Weeks in Florida.

The year 1961 saw another move for the Flight, this time to Horsham St Faith, where in a much depleted state it struggled to survive. As often happens, it is only when things are near extinction that people realise just what it is they are about to lose, and after yet another move in 1963 to Coltishall the two remaining aircraft were rejoined by the Spitfire XIX (PS853). The atmosphere at Coltishall was more conducive to maintaining and running the Flight, and in that first year the three aircraft gave some fifty displays. The Flight also began to grow in numbers again when the next year a Spitfire V (AB910) was donated by Vickers-Armstrong. It was flown to Coltishall by their chief test pilot Jeffrey Quill, who was the same test pilot who had contributed so much to the initial development of the Spitfire.

In 1968 all the aircraft took part in the film *The Battle of Britain*. Research for this film discovered a Spitfire II, P7350, at RAF Colerne in Wiltshire, which was restored to airworthy condition for the film and was subsequently donated to the Flight. This aircraft is significant as it is the only plane owned by the Flight that actually saw action during the Battle of Britain. With these new additions to the fleet the future looked a great deal better, and in 1972 this new-found lease of life was given a further boost when the Hawker Aircraft Company presented to the Flight the last Hurricane built (PZ865 'The Last of the Many') in a completely refurbished state. The Flight now had six unique aircraft and at that time the only two airworthy Hurricanes in the world.

In 1973 the fighters were joined by what at that time was the only airworthy Lancaster in the world (PA474). This aircraft had been recovered from RAF Henlow in 1965 by members of 44 Squadron, then based at Waddington and flying Vulcans. The aircraft was brought to airworthy status for the

The crew of PA474 are briefed prior to a photographic survey flight by a captain of the Royal Engineers. *Left to right*: W/O Charles, Flt Sgt G.J. Stanley (Flight Engineer), -?-, Master Pilot W/O Nutt and Flt Sgt Jim Newman (Navigator). Master Pilot Nutt was allocated to PA474 for most of the detachment, but she was flown on occasion by other pilots. *(Battle of Britain Memorial Flight Archive)*

flight back to Waddington, but once there work commenced to restore the airframe properly. This work continued for the next two years until in 1967 an aircraft that was being restored to take its place in a museum took to the air again, setting a precedent, proving a point and ensuring that the aircraft would now fly on an 'occasional' basis. The rest, as they say, is history!

With the arrival of the Lancaster came a change of name and the Battle of Britain Memorial Flight was born. The formation of Lancaster, Spitfire and Hurricane has now become a familiar and much-

PA474 at Cranfield with the laminar flow test-rig in place. These experiments by Handley Page's research and design engineers into the efficiency of laminar flow wings were in connection with the proposed HP 117, 'a 550mph, 300-seat, all-wing aircraft which will reduce transatlantic fares by 30 per cent'. *(Aeroplane Monthly Archive)*

Opposite: Lancasters of 82 Squadron at RAF Eastleigh, Nairobi, in 1951. PA474 was coded 'M' and may well be in this photograph. They look very different in their peacetime guise, with the lack of turrets and the faired-over rear cockpit and astrodome. *(Battle of Britain Memorial Flight Archive)*

Another view of PA474 at Cranfield with a different wing section in place. Note that she is still coded 'M'. She also continued to sport the 82 Squadron Crest under the cockpit during her stay here. Note also that the pitot tube has been moved from the port-side nose to the starboard wingtip.

(Aeroplane Monthly Archive)

loved sight and sound at air displays throughout the country. It has also added a very fitting living memorial to those thousands of souls who gave their lives while serving in Bomber Command.

In 1976 the Flight moved to what was to become its permanent home at RAF Coningsby, and while the flying and maintenance was still carried out on a 'voluntary' basis they now had a full-time Commanding Officer. Appearances at displays and commemorative events had been increasing all the while, along with request for visits to the Flight, and these demands made the presence of a permanent

Commanding Officer essential. Before long more full-time staff were needed not only to organise the logistics of getting the aircraft to various events on time but also to plan who would fly them and when. Until recently it was accepted that the Commanding Officer was the 'Lancaster Driver', while the rest of the crew and the fighter pilots were volunteers drawn from active squadrons. At weekends time was less of an issue, but during the week many of these pilots struggled to find time to continue their training on piston-engined aircraft. The ground crew were now semi-permanent but they could be called

PA474 minus her mid-upper turret in transit from RAF Kemble to RAF Coltishall after a major service in 1976. A further addition in recent years has been the fairing between the rear turret and the fuselage. This acts as a slipstream deflector and prevents a great deal of buffeting in the rear turret. *(Aeroplane Monthly Archive)*

PZ865 begins to take shape at Langley. The wire-braced tubular space-frame is almost complete, awaiting only the wooden formers and stringers. The method of construction of the Hurricane fuselage was very little changed from the methods employed on the pre-war Hawker Fury and Hart series of aircraft. *(Aeroplane Monthly Archive)*

Mounted on her own undercarriage, with the wooden formers and stringers in place and the Rolls-Royce Merlin mounted, she takes on the familiar shape and aura of a Hurricane. The banner is in place and the theatre of service roll of honour is attached to the tail plane, and if you have sharper eyes than me, you may be able to decipher the message on the engine rocker cover from 'The Back Room Boys'. *(Aeroplane Monthly Archive)*

From the First of the Few
1935-I OF
BRUSSELS EXHIBITION
BATTLE of FRANCE
DUNKIRK
BATTLE of BRITAIN
NARVIK · RUSSIA
IRAN · MALTA
AFRICA · BURMA
SICILY · ITALY
NORMANDY

To the Last of the Thousands
8 GUN FIGHTER
12 GUN FIGHTER
4 CANNON FIGHTER
TANK BUSTER TRAIN BUSTER
FLEET AIR ARM FIGHTER
FIGHTER BOMBER
CATAPULT FIGHTER
METEOROLOGICAL AIRCRAFT

The Last of the Many!

at a moment's notice to serve in the 'Modern Air Force'. Today, much has changed and there are now twenty-three full-time ground crew, not to mention a permanent Warrant Officer Engineering, a Chief Technician and four Operations Managers.

There was a near-tragedy in August 1978 when Spitfire V (AB910) collided with a Harvard while taxiing for take-off for the return transit after a display at Bex in Switzerland. The damage to the Spitfire was substantial, but luckily neither of the aircraft caught fire and the only casualty was the pilot of the Harvard, who managed to break a leg while vacating his aircraft. It was not until 1981 that AB910 finally rejoined the Flight after a complete structural restoration by the Repair and Salvage Squadron at RAF Abingdon.

In 1983 and 1985 respectively the Flight acquired a De Havilland Chipmunk (WK518) from Manston and a De Havilland Devon (VP981) from 207 Squadron. These aircraft were essential to the

The final adjustments: in a few months the cannon were replaced to accommodate extra fuel tanks for air-racing. Farewell pennants in eight different languages hang beneath the main banner. *(Aeroplane Monthly Archive)*

George Bulman, the pilot who had first flown the prototype in 1935, at the controls of PZ865. He usually wore a bowler hat for special occasions such as this. *(Aeroplane Monthly Archive)*

continuation training of aircrew in multi-piston engine and tail-wheel aircraft, the Devon in particular being useful to the Lancaster crews for asymmetric and procedural training. These two aircraft were also used to reconnoitre new display venues and to transport ground crews and essential spares to display sites.

The Flight continued in this format into the 1990s, albeit with ever-increasing demands for their participation at public events; by 1992 participation was up to 150 events and by 1996 it exceeded 500. In 1991, however, Hurricane LF363 was put out of service while in transit to Jersey owing to an engine fire. The pilot, Sqn Ldr Allan 'Slam' Martin,

In her royal blue and gold livery, PZ865 waits to taxi out for the start of the 1950 King's Cup air race. The Hurricane was entered in the race by HRH Princess Margaret and flown by Gp Capt Peter Townsend. During this period the Hurricane still wore the inscription 'The Last of the Many' beneath the cockpit on her port side. *(Aeroplane Monthly Archive)*

attempted a forced landing at RAF Wittering but the
engine failed completely during his approach and he
crash-landed. The aircraft caught fire and was substantially damaged. Fortunately Sqn Ldr Martin escaped
with relatively minor injuries. It was to be seven years,
however, before LF363 returned to the Flight after a
complete rebuild, and in 1994 Spitfire XIX PS853 was
sold to help defray the cost of the work.

In 1993 the Devon was retired and a DC3 Dakota
was obtained from Boscombe Down to fulfil the roles

played by the much-loved De Havilland aircraft. In
a way it is more fitting that the support aircraft for
the Flight is of the same vintage as the rest of the
machines; it is also larger and heavier than the
Devon, therefore giving a closer feel to the Lancaster.
The Dak was found to be substantially non-standard
when it arrived but has gradually been brought back
to a more authentic configuration.

Another Chipmunk (WG486) was acquired in
1995 to add to the training fleet. The two are today

resplendent in an eye-catching high specular black paint scheme and are popular members of the team. The new pilots, most of whom have no piston-engined tail-wheel aircraft experience and carry out their conversion training on these machines, marvel at this little aeroplane's ability to fly sideways and its reaction to every nuance of wind and weather.

The ex-RAF St Athan Museum collection Spitfire IX MK356 arrived at the Flight in November 1997. This aircraft had also spent time as a gate guardian and had appeared, albeit in a static role, in the film *The Battle of Britain*, so it was now among sympathetic friends!

The Flight's final acquisitions were two Spitfire XVIs (TE311 and TB382). Both ex-RAF Exhibition Flight aircraft, they have been allocated to the Flight for use as spares. At the moment a spare fuselage is being constructed from components of both aircraft; this work is being carried out on a part-time basis as a labour of love largely by Chief Technician (CT)

LF363 in company with Spitfire XIX PM631 and assorted classic 'Paraffin Parrots' for the annual Battle of Britain display in September 1960. Note the Ansons and the Beverley in the background. *(Aeroplane Monthly Archive)*

This is LF363 in 1969 wearing the colours of Douglas Bader's aircraft while he was
Commanding Officer of 242 (Canadian) Squadron. His wing commander's pennant can be
seen below the cockpit. *(Aeroplane Monthly Archive)*

Paul Blackah, as time from main commitments allows. Such dedication sums up the atmosphere at the Flight: the ground crew will work every hour God sends to ensure that all the aircraft are absolutely perfect and only then will they permit the aircrew to enjoy the privilege of displaying them.

The Rolls-Royce Merlin and Griffon Engines

In 1933, when Sydney Camm and Reginald Mitchell were evolving their designs that were to become the Hurricane and the Spitfire, Rolls-Royce was in the final stages of designing an aero engine that would represent a significant advance on the Kestrel which powered the Hawker Fury, the premier front-line fighter of the time. Experience gained from the production of the famous 'R' engine that had powered the Supermarine Schneider Trophy winners was put to good use. This new engine, known as the PV 12 (the PV standing for private venture), was to be a 60-degree V12 of 27 litres capacity.

Initial testing was carried out in a Hawker Hart, which was convenient and also allowed the ironing-out of initial teething problems. Both the prototype Hawker Hurricane and the Spitfire flew with this

A sad line-up of Spitfires awaiting the scrap man at RAF Colerne in 1947. P7350 is the first aircraft in the line. *(Norman Parker)*

P7350 on show at the 1959
Battle of Britain display at
RAF Colerne. *(Ron
Cranham)*

After this incident in 1959 at
the OXO cricket ground at
Bromley in Kent, Spitfires
and Hurricanes were
forbidden to lead the annual
Battle of Britain fly-past.
SL574 was rebuilt to static
display condition and for
many years was gate
guardian at RAF Bentley
Priory. For completely
unfounded reasons, this
accident cast doubt on the
use of American-built
Packard Merlins.

engine, which had now become known as the Merlin. By the time these two fighters were in production, however, the engine had already been developed to the point where the Merlin I had been superseded and these aircraft were fitted with the Merlin II or III. It is a strange coincidence that like Reginald Mitchell, Sir Henry Royce, who had been entirely responsible for the Merlin, died before his concept reached fruition.

Right from the start the engine demonstrated its enormous potential for development. However successfully Daimler-Benz or BMW developed their power plants for the Me109 and the Fw190, Rolls-Royce was always able to come up with the answer. In 1941, when the Spitfire V was in production, the Merlin 45 installed in that mark was developing 40 per cent more power than the prototype. By 1944 the engine had been developed to the point

In this photograph AB910 still has her three-bladed propeller, but has been equipped with a PR Mk XI windscreen and canopy for racing by Air Cdre Alan Wheeler at Farnborough. Air Cdre Wheeler was at that time the CO at Farnborough. *(Alan Wheeler via Peter Arnold)*

Jeffrey Quill hands over AB910 and the relevant documentation to Air Marshal 'Zulu' Morris at Coltishall in September 1965. Quill had started operational flying with the Met Flight at RAF Duxford in 1933, later becoming a test pilot for Supermarine. 'Mutt' Summers flew the Spitfire on its maiden flight on 5 March 1936 but Jeffrey Quill flew it just three weeks later to establish performance figures before the aircraft was handed over to A&AEE Martlesham Heath for RAF trials. Jeffrey Quill delivered the first production Spitfire to the RAF at Duxford in 1938 and marked his retirement from test flying at the same airfield on 14 September 1957, when he very fittingly displayed a Mk LFXVI at the Battle of Britain Day display. *(Battle of Britain Memorial Flight Archive)*

Margaret Horton at RAF Coltishall with Sqn Ldr Mike Raw, reliving the memory of her dramatic trip on the tail-plane of AB910 at 53 OTU. *(Battle of Britain Memorial Flight Archive)*

In her blue and gold racing livery, AB910 poses for the camera close to Farnborough in 1949. *(via Peter Arnold)*

On 11 July 1957 three Spitfire PR XIXs flew from Duxford to Biggin Hill to form the Historic Aircraft Flight, in company with the lone Hurricane. They were piloted on this occasion by Gp Capt 'Johnny' Johnson, Gp Capt James Rankin and Wg Cdr Peter Thompson. *(via Peter Arnold)*

where it could produce almost twice the power of the original. From late 1941 many engines were built under licence by Packard in the United States, largely for use in the North American P-51 Mustang.

By 1942 Rolls-Royce realised that there had to be a limit to the development potential of the Merlin and so the Griffon, an engine originally developed for the Fleet Air Arm, was chosen to take its place. The Griffon was similar in design to the Merlin but had a larger capacity of 36.7 litres. This engine was first fitted to the Spitfire XII, and when in the sub-

sequent marks of Spitfire did much to restore the superiority of the Spitfire over the later marks of Fw190.

The Flight has two Hurricanes and three Spitfires powered by Merlins, and two Spitfires powered by Griffons, not to mention the Lancaster, powered by four Merlins. People are inclined to associate the Merlin only with the fighters and they forget that this famous engine powered Lancasters, Halifaxes, Mosquitos and many others. The sound of a Merlin is such that everyone looks up, aware that it is something really special!

PS915 in a line-up at Wahn in 1948. Although the codes are difficult to read in this picture, she is said to be third from the front on the right-hand side, coded OI-K. *(Peter Arnold)*

Energetic WAAFs and MK356 in spurious markings are caught by the MOD PR photographer at Hawkinge on 17 November 1954. *(MOD)*

CHAPTER 3
The Avro Lancaster – PA474

Avro Lancaster PA474 was built to B Mk I reconnaissance standard by Vickers-Armstrong at Chester in 1944–5. She was modified to Far East standard and was to be used with Tiger Force against the Japanese, although she was never used in this role owing to the sudden end of the war in the Far East. She then had all her gun turrets removed and was further modified for use on photographic reconnaissance duties with 82 Squadron in Africa. For this purpose two American K-17 cameras were fitted in the H2S scanner position beneath the fuselage, and at the same time internal supplementary fuel tanks were fitted as the average sortie lasted anything from eight to twelve hours. Between 1948 and 1952 the Lancasters of 82 Squadron were to photograph around one and a quarter million square miles of the African continent, including areas of Gambia,

Opposite page: Lancaster PA474 silhouetted against a summer sky, homeward bound to RAF Coningsby after giving a display at Cranfield in 1987. This shows the aircraft in her element and was one of those happy photographic accidents that sometimes happen beyond what was planned at the briefing. She was turning to join formation on the Harvard camera ship for the main photographic sortie.

PA474, flown by Sqn Ldr Tony Banfield, is photographed from the Falcons' Hercules over the English Channel.

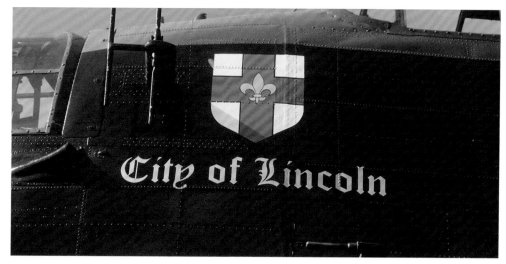

Left: PA474 coded AJ-G to represent the Lancaster flown by Wg Cdr Guy Gibson when he led 617 Squadron on the famous raid on the Ruhr dams in 1943. During each major refurbishment PA474 is repainted to represent an aircraft that was exceptionally long-serving or was flown by a particularly brave crew. Below the cockpit is the coat of arms of the City of Lincoln. PA474 was adopted by the city in March 1975 to commemorate the long association between Lincolnshire and Bomber Command. Here, piloted by Sqn Ldr C.S.M. 'Scott' Anderson MBE, she is on her way to RAF Coningsby from RAF Manston in Kent.

Above: The City of Lincoln coat of arms.

Below: No opportunity is missed to overfly Lincoln and its impressive cathedral.

PA474 pictured en route to RAF Coningsby from RAF Abingdon on a gloomy day in 1984 after a major overhaul. During this work she was repainted in the colours of 101 Squadron and coded SR-D.

Bechuanaland, Southern Rhodesia, Northern Rhodesia, Kenya, Uganda, Gold Coast, Nyasaland and Tanganyika.

In May 1952 PA474 was passed to Flight Refuelling Ltd (a company formed by Sir Alan Cobham, the man who had been very much responsible for popularising aviation in pre-war Britain) for conversion to pilotless drone status. She remained with the company for the next year and a half, and although a great deal of design work on the project was carried out, no actual physical conversion work

was completed. It was then decided that the Avro Lincoln was better suited to the role of target drone, so PA474 was given a reprieve.

March 1954 saw the Lancaster moved to Cranfield for conversion into a flying test-bed for experiments into the behaviour of laminar flow wings. For this purpose a mounting frame was constructed inside the fuselage to support a wing section above the fuselage midway between the astrodome and the tail-plane. In addition, hydraulic rams to change the angle of incidence of the test wing in flight and a system for introducing coloured dyes into the airflow over the test wing were also added. The mind boggles at the thought of trying to land this contraption in any sort of significant cross-wind. Nevertheless PA474 fulfilled this role until lack of readily available spares, especially Merlin engines, made it impossible to continue, and she was once again superseded by the Avro Lincoln and was passed to MOD Air Historical Branch (RAF) to be restored to her original specification for display at the proposed Royal Air Force Museum at Hendon. She was stored in the open along with Avro Lincoln RF398 at RAF Henlow (the hangar being too small to accommodate the wing-span of these aircraft) and was left to face the vagaries of the weather and to help any birds that needed a new home! A change of fortune, however, was just around the corner.

At that time 44 Squadron was based at RAF Waddington operating the Avro Vulcan. Its Commanding Officer, Wg Cdr D'Arcy, was an enthusiastic aviation historian. Aware that his squadron, while based at RAF Waddington in 1941, had been the first to receive and operate the Lancaster, he was on the look-out for a suitable Lancaster airframe to display at the station. He detailed three squadron members to help in this search, one of whom was Sqn Ldr Leach BA, RAF, who was to become one of the prime movers in getting PA474 back into the air. He later wrote a detailed history of the aircraft, *A Lancaster at Peace*.

The search revealed several Lancasters in such diverse locations as France and New Caledonia. For various reasons these were deemed unsuitable and it appeared that out of the 7,377 Lancasters built,

The Lancaster takes part in many important memorial events. Here she is seen from the telegraphist/air gunner's position in the Royal Navy Historic Flight's Fairey Swordfish during the rehearsal for the fly-past during the 40th anniversary commemorations of the Normandy landings. The requirement was for the two aircraft to overfly the saluting base in formation, which, owing to the disparity in speeds between the two machines, proved to be no small problem. With the Lancaster flying as slowly as was comfortable, and the Swordfish as fast as possible, the run-in to the formation point was started 4 miles out with the Swordfish 2 miles ahead of the Lancaster. For a brief moment the two aircraft were in formation over the saluting base.

there was not one that could be found to suit the purpose of 44 Squadron. It was at this gloomy point that someone mentioned that a Lancaster, in company with a Lincoln, was standing on the grass at RAF Henlow!

It appeared that this particular airframe, after restoration, would be ideal for the purpose the members of 44 Squadron had in mind. They knew that the Air Historical Branch wanted the aircraft to go into a museum but when it was discovered that the actual opening of the Royal Air Force Museum was still some years away, Wg Cdr D'Arcy successfully argued that PA474 would be better served by being kept in a dry environment in a hangar at RAF Waddington. Also, while in this environment further restoration work could more easily be carried out. Permission for the move was eventually granted and the aircraft was surveyed prior to being dismantled for her move by road to Lincolnshire. During this survey it was established that the aircraft was in fact in very good condition and that there was nothing wrong that could not be easily diagnosed and rectified. The engines in particular, having been properly inhibited before storage, were in a remarkably good state of preservation.

Further negotiations now ensued to convince the Air Historical Branch and the MOD that it would be better to fly the Lancaster to RAF Waddington rather than dismantle her for a trip by road. Permission was eventually granted for one flight only, and work began to restore her for this purpose. It was during this period that the Lincoln was 'robbed' of its tail-wheel unit to replace the unserviceable item on the Lancaster. This unit is still in place today.

Three views of the Normandy coast from the mid-upper turret of the Lancaster in June 1984. Sitting in this turret is like riding on top of an express train.

On 18 August 1965, in company with a Vickers Varsity full of gentlemen of the press, PA474 took off from RAF Henlow for the trip north. After a couple of low-level fly-pasts at Henlow, the Lancaster joined the Varsity for an air-to-air photographic session and after this broke off to over fly RAF Scampton, leaving the Varsity to land at RAF Waddington, allowing the press photographers time to position themselves for the arrival of the Lancaster. Apart from an interesting take-off from the grass at Henlow, the entire flight was completed without incident. The first phase of PA474's new life had begun.

Once again, the shadow of a Lancaster races across the Normandy countryside.

On the way home from the D-Day 40th anniversary commemorations, the Battle of Britain Memorial Flight flies over HMS *Scylla* as she drops anchor off St Helier in Jersey. Taken from the open loading ramp of an RAF Hercules, this shot was set up by the navigator on the Lancaster, Flt Lt Dick Cave, who, having served on secondment to the Royal Navy, had 'contacts'! All of this was made possible by the Flight's precise timing and the cooperation of the commander of HMS *Scylla*. The pilot of the Hercules gave me a running commentary as the moment approached; for obvious reasons, I couldn't see what was about to appear in front of me.

The transit flights to and from the annual Battle of Britain air displays in the Channel Islands are an excellent opportunity for air-to-air photography. This picture was taken on the way home in 1985. The course to the mainland dictates that one is shooting into the light, but some interesting effects can be obtained. This back-lit image of the Lancaster just off the coast of Guernsey is evocative of moonlight operations in 1943.

Over the Channel in 1986 the Lancaster breaks away from the camera aircraft to make her way home. She is wearing 101 Squadron markings and this is an apt location as 101 Squadron was employed in counter-measure operations over the Channel on the eve of D-Day dropping 'Window' (large bundles of metal foil) to confuse enemy radar during the build-up to the actual landings.

Looking remarkably like her ill-starred predecessor the Avro Manchester, PA474 formates on the Andover allocated to the RAF's parachute team, the Falcons. As the Falcons and the Battle of Britain Memorial Flight attend some of the same displays, it is sometimes possible to arrange to use their Andover as a camera platform without incurring extra flying hours on either aircraft. The Lancaster pilot, Sqn Ldr Tony Banfield, is confident enough to bring the Lanc close in to the ramp of the Andover – close enough to see the reflection of the Andover in the bomb-aimer's Perspex blister.

'Mike Squared', based at RAF Elsham Wolds, was one of the most famous and long-serving Lancasters of the Second World War. Delivered originally to 103 Squadron, with which she completed 66 sorties, she was then transferred to 576 Squadron, where she completed another 65. Then she went back to 103 Squadron for a further 9! When she was withdrawn from service in December 1944 she had completed some 974 operational hours. Here, PA474 pays tribute to this aircraft and her crews. The members of 576 Squadron referred to her as 'Mike Squared', while 103 Squadron knew her as 'Mother of them all'.

Still minus its nose and mid-upper gun turrets, the Lancaster lacked the familiar outline of an operational aircraft, and a search began for these items. At the same time a complete and thorough survey was carried out to establish exactly what engineering work still needed to be carried out to complete the restoration. One of the first jobs was to give the aircraft an identity in keeping with her new home, so she was given the codes KM-B in honour of Sqn Ldr John Nettleton's aircraft which took part in the raid on the MAN engine works at Augsburg in April 1942. His was the only Lancaster from 44 Squadron to return to RAF Waddington, and for his actions during this raid he was subsequently awarded the Victoria Cross. After a period away from the squadron, he was to return as Commanding Officer, only to be shot down and killed in July 1943 during a raid on Turin.

Opposite: Sgt Ian Davies, aided by Cpls Mark Arnold and Nigel Bunn, keep a close ear and eye on the Lancaster and the Dakota as they start up to leave Jersey States Airport for the annual Battle of Britain display at Guernsey.

At present the Lancaster represents EE176 of 61 Squadron. Coded QR-M, this aircraft was christened 'Mickey the Moocher' and was one of only a few operational Lancasters to top the 100-mission mark, surviving 15 missions to Berlin and over 100 raids on most of the other major Bomber Command targets of the Second World War.

The plaque next to the door of the Lancaster commemorates all who served in Bomber Command, and especially the many thousands who made the supreme sacrifice for their country.

Close inspection before each flight is the rule rather than the exception at the Flight. All the ground crew take great pride in their work and there is a definite feeling that the aircrew have the aircraft 'on loan' and they dare not bring one back in anything other than pristine condition. Here Cpl Mark Arnold inspects the exhaust stubs on the Lancaster for any problems. The ground crew fly in the Lancaster to the display venues and it is highly likely that Mark has heard something on the way to the Channel Islands that he thinks warrants closer inspection.

The Lancaster is kept in immaculate condition.

Opposite: Cpl Clive O'Connell puts his back into releasing the bar from the tow tractor at RAF Coningsby for an early morning start to a weekend of displays.

62

The exhaust deposits from the Lancaster's starboard inner engine over the upper surface of the wing give some idea of the problem involved in keeping her pristine. Multiply this by four and it is obviously some cleaning operation!

Taxiing at RAF Coningsby with the engines perfectly in sync!

While all this was going on, the search for the gun turrets continued. A front turret was located in use as a gate guardian by an ATC unit in Haverhill. They were prepared to part with it only in exchange for some suitably eye-catching piece of hardware to put in its place. A dummy Fireflash missile was soon located and the deal was done! Having been left standing in the open for many years it was feared that the turret could not be made serviceable, but after a thorough inspection the armourers at RAF Waddington thought otherwise; the biggest problem was the replacement Perspex glazing panels which had become crazed and cracked over the years. Using the original sections of Perspex as patterns, new moulds were manufactured, and after some failures replacement panels were produced. The mid-upper turret, though, was proving far more difficult to locate. Finally, in January 1967, Mr Wortley (who

Having come to a halt, the signal to cut the engines is given by the member of ground crew acting as marshal.

The Frazer Nash FN121 rear turret. The rear navigation light remains in place but the original 'Village Inn' gun-laying radar is no longer fitted. Wartime Lancasters had 'Monica' tail-warning radar in this position as well. In the centre of the turret glazing can be seen the sliding clear vision panel. When this is open it gives just enough room to get one's camera and head and shoulders through, giving clear vision and a good angle of view.

The centre fuselage of the Lancaster, showing the Frazer Nash FN150 turret that was located at a gunnery school in Argentina and shipped to England aboard HMS *Hampshire*. The fairing around the turret acts as a cam, on which can be seen the wheeled arm that prevents the guns being depressed to the point where the gunner shoots down his own aircraft.

had taken it upon himself to locate a turret) contacted the engineers to say that one had been found in good condition in Argentina and was at that moment aboard HMS *Hampshire* on its way to England. Upon arrival it was found to be ideal and was packed away to await the fitting of the 'taboo track' to the fuselage. (The taboo track is the fairing around the turret that prevents the guns being depressed to the point where the gunner can hit his own aircraft.) It was to be a further eight years before this work could be completed. In the meantime further restoration work went ahead and the aircraft slowly but surely began to look like a proper Lancaster!

The new station commander at RAF Waddington, Gp Capt Arthur Griffiths, was an enthusiastic supporter of all this work and it was he who was largely responsible for gaining the permission of the Air Historical Branch for a post-restoration test flight to take place. This was no easy task as the AHB had been given to believe that the 'one flight only' restoration at RAF Henlow would end in restoration at RAF Waddington to static museum standard only. However, this test flight took place in November 1967 and was a great success, so much so that with further lobbying and persuasion permission was granted for PA474 to make 'occasional' flights. These were to become more frequent and ambitious and soon the public began to expect that the Lancaster would appear at commemorative fly-pasts and the Battle of Britain displays. Any opposition to the project now turned to qualified support, and PA474 now took up its new roles, not only as a living

The Frazer Nash FN5 front turret was recovered from the Haverhill ATC Squadron in exchange for a dummy Fireflash missile. Beneath the turret is the bomb-aimer's blister with its circular 'optical flat' in front of the actual bomb sight.

Above: Lancaster PA474 above the English Channel in 2002, returning from Jersey to RAF Coningsby. The escape hatches have been removed in an attempt to give the crew some air conditioning. In fine weather the temperature in the Lanc, especially inside the cockpit, rises to almost unbearable levels.

Right: The Lancaster carries out a low pass on her return home from a display. There are always people at the fence or watching from a convenient lay-by, hoping for a treat such as this. Sometimes at weekends there are upwards of a hundred people watching and waiting. The ground crew regularly find time to have a chat with them and hand out brochures.

The Lancaster is powered by four Rolls-Royce Merlin V12 27-litre engines, each rated at about 1,280hp at 3,000rpm for take-off. The start-up sequence of the engines on the Lanc is 3, 4, 2 and 1. This gives safe access to the engines for the ground crew in the event of an engine catching fire on start-up. No. 3 engine is always started first as it is this engine that drives the air compressor that works the brakes and radiator shutters, as well as the hydraulic pumps. The exhausts on PA474 no longer carry their flame-damping shrouds. The carburettor air intake with its mesh anti-ice guard can be seen just forward of the leading edge of the wing.

Sqn Ldr Paul Day OBE, AFC, has his arm twisted by visitors to say nice things about the Lancaster! Paul was with the Flight for twenty-four seasons and has amassed over 1,000 hours on Spitfires and Hurricanes. He is a fighter pilot, having flown Hawker Hunters, F-4 Phantoms and Tornados, and as such maintains a somewhat disparaging attitude towards 'the bomber'. At times he had to fly in 'the bomber' and likened it to 'watching paint dry' or similar. He also has a healthy and deep-seated dislike for aesthetically displeasing aircraft with 'round engines'!

memorial to the 55,000 aircrew who died in Bomber Command during the Second World War, but also as a premier air display attraction!

In November 1973 PA474 joined the Spitfires and Hurricanes of the Historic Aircraft Flight at RAF Coltishall to form what was to become known as the Battle of Britain Memorial Flight. The restoration work that had been started by the enthusiasts at RAF Waddington was now put on a more formal footing, as were the Lancaster's displays. She was now carrying out some seventy displays a year, and work is still continuing to restore her to 'as built' condition.

In March 1976 the whole Flight moved north to RAF Coningsby, which would be its home for the next thirty years. The fine tuning of details on the

aircraft continues and the enthusiasm for the task has grown, with each new set of pilots and engineers bringing their own particular brand of pride, love and obsession to the Flight.

The Lancaster is at home here in Lincolnshire, more commonly known as Bomber County. She is a much-loved sight as she completes some 150 displays a year. As she goes about her duties, she has become a magnificent tribute to all those who gave their all in Bomber Command.

Since 2000 the Lancaster has worn the markings of a Lancaster from 61 Squadron, known as 'Mickey the Moocher'. The original aircraft, coded QR-M, completed some 125 missions and actually survived the war, only to meet an ignominious end at the hands of a scrapman.

The Lancaster flies a practice display as the ground crew play volleyball. You can be sure, though, that they all have one ear alert to any missed beat of the Merlins.

With PZ865 standing off to starboard, the Lancaster thunders over Sark on her way to Jersey in September 2002.

CHAPTER 4

The Hawker Hurricanes – LF363 and PZ865

The Battle of Britain Flight operates two Hawker Hurricane IIcs, of which LF363 is the oldest. Her exact history is not altogether clear as there are unrecorded gaps and also records of her presence at various locations that don't quite tally with other accounts of her activities. Like the Lancaster, she owes her existence to the dedication of a small band of enthusiasts within the RAF who were determined to keep the legend alive.

LF363 was built as part of contract no. L 62305 as a Mk IIc fitted with bomb racks, at Langley in Buckinghamshire. She first flew on 1 January 1944 and at the end of that month was ferried to 5 MU at RAF Kemble. From there, in March, she moved to 63 Squadron at Turnhouse and subsequently, in May, to

The longest serving aircraft in the Flight is Hurricane LF363, seen here over a sun-dappled Cambridgeshire countryside coded GN-A to represent a Hurricane I from 249 Squadron based at RAF North Weald in 1940. This was one of the main defending squadrons involved in 'Eagle Day'.

Hurricane LF363 at readiness for a trip from Barkston Heath, where the Flight was based during 2003 while the runway at Coningsby was replaced to the standards required for the Eurofighter. She is coded US-C, in honour of a Mk I Hurricane from 56 Squadron in 1940 when the squadron was based at North Weald.

Sqn Ldr Alan Martin was lucky to escape this accident at RAF Wittering without serious injury. LF363 was in transit between RAF Coningsby and the Channel Islands in September 1991 when the engine began to run rough and smoke poured from the exhausts. He tried to make an emergency landing at the airfield, but on his final approach the engine quit completely and with a cockpit full of smoke and fuel vapour it crashed and burned out. The aircraft was rebuilt and returned to the Flight in 1998. *(Battle of Britain Memorial Flight Archive)*

309 (Polish) Squadron at Drem, wearing the codes WC-H. Records show, however, that she remained on the move and between the middle and the end of 1944 she was variously listed as being at 22 MU (Silloth), 63 Squadron, 26 Squadron and once again at 22 MU. Other reports seem to indicate that she was in fact based at 22 MU for the whole of that period.

In August 1945 she was listed as being with 62 Operational Training Unit and after that again at 22 MU. She was then moved to Middle Wallop, where she remained until being struck off charge in June 1947. In August of that year however, she reappeared on Fighter Command's Communication Squadron and later that year as part of the Station Flight at Thorney Island, an airfield that was part of 11 Group. The AOC 11 Group was Air Cdre Vincent, who had commanded RAF Northolt during the Battle of Britain, and it was probably due to him that LF363 survived. He was determined that the aircraft should be kept in an airworthy condition so as to be able to lead the annual Battle of Britain Day fly-past.

Sqn Ldr Paul Day gives the benefit of his experience to Flt Lt Jack Hamill as he prepares for his first flight in a Hurricane.

Flt Lt 'Merv' Payne flies LF363 on a bleak day over the Lincolnshire countryside. She is painted in the matt black colours of 85 Squadron when operating as a night fighter unit.

The Hurricane's rear fuselage and tail-plane, showing the mixture of materials used in the manufacture of this machine.

Flt Lt Peter Bouch gets in close to the rear turret of the Lancaster in LF363. Transits to and from displays are flown strictly under Visual Flight Rules at 2,000 feet and at around 175mph. Very occasionally, given exactly the correct weather conditions, they can be persuaded to fly above well-broken cloud for photographic purposes.

In late 1948 she was taken back to Langley for engineering work to be carried out but remained there pretty much neglected until once again Air Cdre Vincent became involved, sending fitters from Thorney Island to get her airworthy again. Unfortunately, in 1949, at the end of the ferry flight back to Thorney Island, she made a wheels-up landing on the grass and sustained considerable damage. Maintenance personnel at Thorney Island managed to repair the aircraft in time for that year's Battle of Britain fly-past. Later that year Thorney Island closed as a fighter base and the resident squadrons, along with LF363, moved to RAF Water-beach, from where she continued to operate. She was grounded again in 1953 after an incident involving the loss of her cockpit canopy in flight. No other damage was incurred and a new canopy was finally found in 1954.

The next year LF363 went back to Hawkers at Langley for a major overhaul, during which her cannon stub fairings were removed. She emerged from Hawkers in 1957 in 'as new' condition and went to Biggin Hill to join the two Spitfire XIXs. After many new homes, these three aircraft were to become the founder members of the Battle of Britain Memorial Flight at RAF Coltishall.

Over the years, as well as fulfilling her normal display duties, LF363 has also starred in four major films: *Angels One Five*, *Reach for the Sky*, *The One That Got Away* and *The Battle of Britain*. She also led a Spitfire in a fly-past over Bladen Cemetery in a final salute to Sir Winston Churchill in 1965.

In 1991 there was almost total disaster while LF363 was in transit from RAF Coningsby to the Channel Islands, piloted by Sqn Ldr Alan 'Slam' Martin. Close to RAF Wittering the engine began to

LF363 above a typical English rural landscape on a Sunday afternoon. I find it interesting, and very heartening, to note the many village cricket matches.

Flown by Wg Cdr Ron Shimmons, LF363 'enjoys herself' over the Bristol Channel en route to RNAS Culdrose for the annual display in 1987.

Opposite: Sqn Ldr Clive Rowley crosses the Scottish Borders in LF363 on the way to Edinburgh. This was one of those weekends when the weather did its utmost to spoil things but the Flight, through various changes of plan, nevertheless managed to fulfill all its obligations. Hurricane LF363 is resplendent in her new colours for the 2006 season, representing the personal aircraft of Harold 'Birdy' Bird-Wilson of 17 Squadron during the Battle of Britain. Astonishingly, 17 Squadron was one of the few squadrons to fight all the way through without a rest, operating out of Tangmere and Debden. Bird-Wilson's personal emblem of three vengeful swords in pursuit of a Nazi swastika and eagle was thought up after he shot down a Ju88 off Selsey.

This shot of the tail-wheel assembly shows just what an intricate piece of engineering it actually is.

Sqn Ldr Clive Rowley fires up LF363's Merlin with the traditional cloud of white smoke.

Opposite: Flying over the Scottish Borders on a rather overcast day, LF363 shows off the rather unusual wavy demarcation between the sky underside and the camouflaged upper surfaces.

Clive Rowley in LF363 joins
Ian Smith in AB910 for a
formation photograph during
the transit from Coningsby to
Edinburgh.

Spitfire AB910 and Hurricane
LF363 formate on the open
door of the Flight's Dakota.

run very rough and smoke poured into the cockpit. Sqn Ldr Martin was established on finals for a forced landing when the engine quit completely, resulting in a crash on the airfield. Luckily the pilot survived the accident but LF363 caught fire and that her days could have been over – not least because of the cost of rebuilding her. Seven years later, after the sale of one of the Spitfire XIXs to cover the cost of the restoration and a great deal of hard work, in 1998 she rejoined the Flight, wearing very appropriate markings derived from 56 Squadron when they were stationed at North Weald in 1940. She wore the codes US-C and the inscription 'A Phoenix Rising from the Ashes'. From the beginning of the 2006 season she carried the markings of a machine from 17 Squadron that was flown by Flg Off Harold Bird Wilson during the Battle of Britain.

PZ865, the second Hawker Hurricane owned and operated by the Flight, was also built at Langley in 1944 as part of the same contract that produced LF363, and she was the last of 14,233 Hurricanes to be built. In answer to the film *The First of the Few*

(the story of Reginald Mitchell and the Spitfire), she bore the inscription 'The Last of the Many' on her fuselage beneath the cockpit. After her roll-out, at which ceremony she was flanked by a Hawker Hart and a Hawker Tempest, she was test-flown by George Bulman, who had flown the prototype Hurricane on its maiden flight on 6 November 1935. Almost immediately after construction the Hawker Aircraft Company bought PZ865 from the Ministry of Aircraft Construction for use as a test and communications aircraft. After the war, still in Hawker ownership, she was given a new livery of royal blue with gold trim and registered as G-AMAU. Her cannon were removed and extra fuel tanks were fitted in their place. In this configuration she appeared at air displays and was entered in air races; flown by Gp Capt Peter Townsend she was placed second in the King's Cup Air Race at Wolverhampton in 1950.

In the 1960s PZ865 reverted to her original camouflage finish and was used in target-towing trials with the Hawker Sea Fury and as a chase aircraft during the development of the Hawker P1127 Kestrel (the forerunner of the Harrier).

Wg Cdr John Ward in PZ865 over the flat Lincolnshire countryside in November 1985 on the way home to RAF Coningsby after celebrating the 50th anniversary of the first flight of the Hawker Hurricane at Brooklands. The picture shows well the difference in textures denoting either alloy or fabric covering. Sgt Dave Payne, one of the BBMF ground crew, described her as 'basically a biplane with the top wing ripped off'!

Above: PZ865, flown by Flt Lt Paul Rickard, leads Spitfire IIb P7350, piloted by Sqn Ldr Paul Day, home to RAF Coningsby over the Suffolk countryside.

Left: The mask for the famous inscription is applied during the change of markings to celebrate the Hurricane's 50th birthday in 1985 . . . and the end result in the evening light.

Hurricane PZ865 and Spitfire
PR Mk XIX display their very
different profiles to the
camera.

Spitfire PR XIX PS915, and Hurricane IIc PZ865 are refuelled after the display in Jersey ready for their return to RAF Coningsby the following day.

PZ865, flown by Paul Rickard, peels away from Paul Day in Spitfire P7350, showing the very different plan form of the aircrafts' wings.

Like every other available Hurricane or Spitfire, in 1968 she appeared in the film *The Battle of Britain*.

In 1971, after spending some time in the Hawker Museum, PZ865 was given a complete overhaul to bring her up to airworthy condition and in March 1972 she was presented to the Memorial Flight at RAF Coltishall. She has appeared in many different squadron markings during her time with the Flight, including her original factory finish which was applied to celebrate the 50th anniversary of the Hurricane in 1985. She has also appeared in the desert camouflage applied to the aircraft of 261 Squadron and in the colours of 5 Squadron during their service in South East Asia Command. Since 2005 she has appeared in the colours of a Hurricane from 1 (F) Squadron flown by the Czech pilot Flt Lt Karel Kuttelwascher on night intruder operations during 1942.

The Hurricane has somehow always been overshadowed by the Spitfire despite the fact that more of them took part in the Battle of Britain. It was a wonderfully stable gun platform, was easier to fly and took its place in every theatre during the Second World War. With its mixed construction, it was also the true link between the pre-war fighters like the Fury and the stressed-skin construction of the Typhoon, Tempest, Sea Fury, Sea Hawk, Hunter and Harrier. They all bear the glorious name Hawker and were all designed by Sir Sydney Camm!

The nose of Hurricane PZ865. Note the collector ring on top of the fuselage behind the spinner that prevents any oil from the constant speed unit being drawn into the airflow and being deposited on the windscreen.

Compare the design and finish between the Spitfire and the Hurricane.

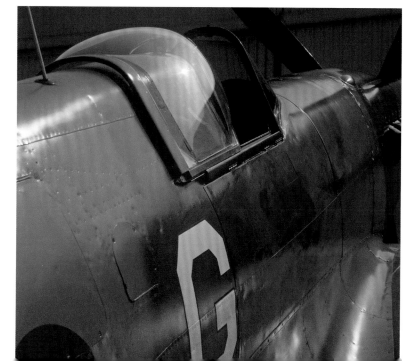

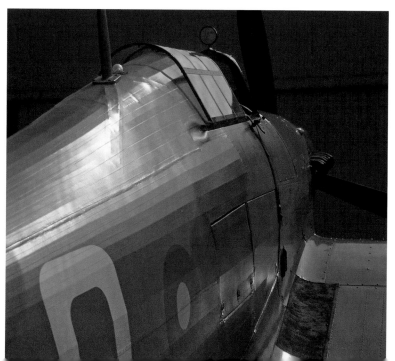

The handgrip used to aid the pilot as he clambers up the wing and into the cockpit.

Sqn Ldr 'Shiney' Simmons, flying PZ865 at eye level for the camera, during his eighth season with the Flight. He is a Qualified Flying Instructor on Tucanos at RAF Linton-on-Ouse. This view of the Hurricane emphasises the large ventral radiator and the thick wing section of the aeroplane.

As the sun glints on the propeller manufacturer's label, 'Shiney' Simmons gets up close to the rear turret of the Lancaster. This picture was shot on a standard lens, which gives an idea of how close he really was. These pilots are the best. All have thousands of hours of flying experience, and know their own limits and those of the pilot of the camera aircraft. All photography is fully briefed on the ground before take-off and all instructions in the air from the photographer to the subject are given by hand signals.

PZ865 in fine weather over the flat Lincolnshire countryside. She wears the SEAC markings, with the small blue and white roundel in evidence. The red in the roundel was dispensed with in this theatre of war to avoid confusion with the red Japanese 'meatball'.

Opposite: PZ865 in SEAC markings, mid-Channel, and the weather conditions look very much like the conditions in the Far East. This sort of thing obviously cannot be planned for and is a gift. I used to envy the photographers taking air-to-air pictures in California with their blessing of consistently good weather, but have learned to love the ever-changing weather patterns of the British Isles.

Hawker Hurricane PZ865 is at present in the colours of a Mk IIc machine that was flown from RAF Tangmere on night intruder missions during 1942 by Karel Kuttelwascher of 1 (F) Squadron. His aircraft was adorned with his personal emblem of a scythe and a banner which read 'Night Reaper', an altogether appropriate name. Below the cockpit on the port side of the aircraft are the swastikas recording eleven of his victories.

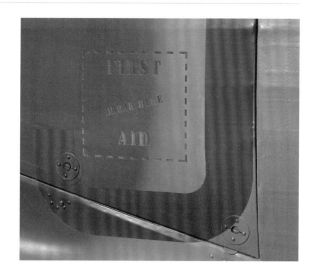

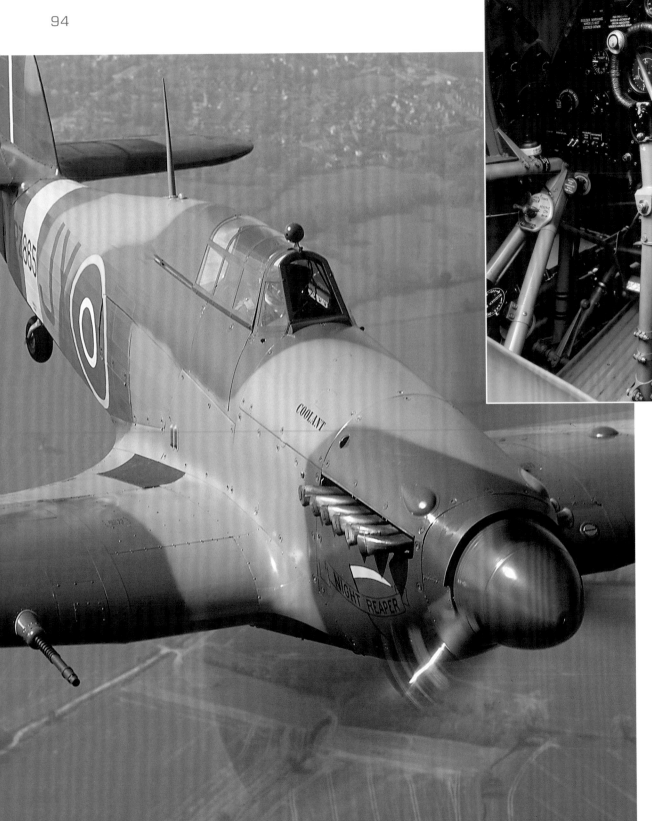

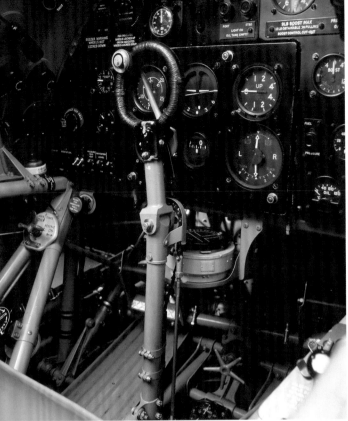

Above: The 'front office' of PZ865.

Three in-flight views of PZ865 during a transit to the first display of the season in March 2005. She was being flown by Wg Cdr Russ Alchorne, and this was his first 'operational' sortie in the Hurricane.

PATCH TO INSIDE
OF LINE ONLY

DO NOT FORGET
TO CHECK
PULL-DOWN STEP

CHAPTER 5

The Supermarine Spitfires – P7350, AB910, MK356, PM631 and PS915

T he Battle of Britain Memorial Flight is in the enviable position of owning five airworthy Spitfires with traceable and important provenance, ranging from a Mk IIa to two Mk XIXs.

Spitfire IIa P7350 is the oldest airworthy Spitfire in the world. She was the fourteenth machine built at Castle Bromwich (out of a total of 11,939) and she first flew in August 1940. She served in the Battle of Britain with 266 (Rhodesia) Squadron and also with 603 (City of Edinburgh) Squadron. It was with the latter, in October 1940, that she took part in a defensive patrol during which she was engaged in combat with an Me109. She was damaged and forced to crash-land. Remarkably, she was repaired in just three weeks by 1 Civilian Repair Unit at Cowley, after which she was sent to 37 MU at Burtonwood, where she was stored until March 1941. (The patches that were used to cover the damage to the wings during this repair are still in evidence on the aircraft today.)

P7350 was then issued to 616 (County of South Yorkshire) Squadron at Tangmere, where she stayed until April, when another move saw her with 64 Squadron at Hornchurch. Yet another move was in store for her, however, as in May the squadron moved to Turnhouse. It was here that her front-line

Wg Cdr John Ward flies P7350 on the way to Eastleigh (Southampton) to celebrate the 50th birthday of the Spitfire. This image of an early mark of Spitfire in its true element emphasises the absence of straight lines anywhere in Reginald Mitchell's design.

On 5 March 1986 P7350 forms up with a PR Mk XI (PL983) and a Mk Ia (AR213) for the fly-past at Eastleigh as the finale to the 50th anniversary celebrations. The event was dogged by bad weather, but a break appeared in the clouds for just long enough to complete the fly-past.

Another view of the formation struggling round the edge of the murk over Southampton! PL983 was at that time owned and flown by Roland Fraissinet. AR213 was owned by the Hon. Patrick Lindsay and flown by Tony Bianchi of Personal Plane Services, based at Booker.

operational life came to an end and she was sent to
Scottish Aviation Ltd at Prestwick for a complete
overhaul. Afterwards she moved to 37 MU again,
where she was stored until April 1942.

The next home for P7350 was the gunnery school
at Sutton Bridge, from where, after an accident in
February 1943, she went to Air Service Training Ltd
at Hamble for repair and again went into storage for
a short time at 6 MU at RAF Brize Norton before
being issued to 57 Operational Training Unit (OTU)
on 31 March. A further visit to Hamble followed
another accident in April 1944, after which she was

taken to RAF Colerne, where she remained until the
end of the war.

At the end of hostilities P7350 was sold as scrap
to the metal dealers John Dale Ltd for £25! It was
fortuitous that someone in the company examined
her logbooks and realised the historical importance
of the airframe, and she was duly presented to the
RAF to become part of the embryo museum being
formed at RAF Colerne.

In 1968 the epic film *The Battle of Britain* came
to her rescue and she was refurbished to airworthy
condition by Simpson Aero Services at RAF Henlow.

How the weather can change in the course of an hour. P7350 in her element on the way home from Southampton in 2006 after the Spitfire 50th anniversary celebrations. She is being flown by Wg Cdr John Ward.

An early morning start in 1985 to get to RNAS Culdrose in good time. This sort of patchy low mist and cloud, together with the acute angle of light, is a gift for photographers.

A February afternoon at RAF Coningsby and a cold one at that! P7350 securely chocked and her tail tied down, as the ground crew carry out ground-running in 1986. The tall silhouette of Engine Trade Manager, Sgt Dave Payne, is in evidence.

On completion of filming she was returned to the Royal Air Force and subsequently presented to the Battle of Britain Memorial Flight at Coltishall. During her long service with the Flight she has appeared in many representative markings. At present she is coded XT-D (City of Edinburgh) Squadron Auxiliary Air Force, but has also worn BA-Y 'The Old Lady' (a presentation aircraft from the Bank of England) and EB-Z of 41 Squadron, the markings of another presentation aircraft from the members of the Royal Observer Corps.

Among those 'in the know' the Mk Vb Spitfire, AB910, is regarded as the best of all the Flight's Spitfires to fly. Built at Castle Bromwich by Vickers-Armstrong in 1941, she was delivered to 222 (Natal) Squadron at North Weald in August that year. Sadly, she was an accident-prone aircraft and a mere two weeks after delivery she was at Air Service Training

Ltd (Exeter) for repairs, after which she went into storage at 37 MU at Burtonwood.

AB910 next saw service with 130 (Punjab) Squadron, but by January 1942 she was under repair at Westland Aircraft Ltd after yet another mishap. Storage at 6 MU at RAF Brize Norton followed, until she was issued to 133 (Eagle) Squadron at Lympne in June. On 19 August, during the Dieppe raid, she was flown on three of the four support patrols mounted by the squadron. On the third patrol she was flown by Flt Sgt 'Dixie' Alexander, who shot down a Dornier Do217 near Dieppe.

In September that year AB910 was transferred to 242 (Canadian) Squadron, coded KV, and two months later, after yet another accident, was to be found at 2 MU at Kirkbride. After this repair there

Flt Lt Jim Wild flies AB910 straight down the middle at RAF Coningsby just before the break to the downwind leg of the circuit before landing. This is the sort of gentle showing off that all pilots enjoy.

followed service with 416 (RCAF) and 402 (RCAF) Squadrons. Her front-line operational service ended in July 1944 when she was transferred to 53 OTU at Kirton-in-Lindsay. It was while operating out of their diversion field at Hilbaldstow that the most amazing episode in the life of AB910 occurred. LACW Margaret Horton was sitting on the tail-plane to hold it down in rough weather while the pilot taxied to the runway. Unaware that she was still on the tail-plane, he turned on to the runway and began his take-off run before she could dismount. Once air-borne, with Margaret still clinging desperately to the

tail, the pilot soon realised that something was amiss, so he completed a somewhat curtailed circuit and landed. A very shaken but otherwise intact Margaret climbed down. The lady in question has in fact visited AB910 since the aircraft has been with the Flight!

The last two units to which AB910 was allocated during hostilities were both radar calibration units, one at RAF Digby and the other at RAF Watton in Norfolk, from where she went to 29 MU in May 1945 to await disposal. She was destined to be broken up, but was bought by Gp Capt Alan

Wheeler for £200. She was sent to Vickers at Swindon for a complete overhaul and emerged from there in a metallic blue livery and coded for the civilian register as G-AISU. After being tuned for air racing, she was flown by Alan Wheeler in Royal Aero Club races at Elmdon and Kemsley, and was entered in King's Cup air races by the ex-ATA pilot Becky Sharpe. In the 1950 King's Cup Sharpe in AB910 raced against Peter Townsend in what was to become the Flight's second Hurricane, PZ865.

Another landing accident put AB910 back with Vickers-Armstrong for repairs, after which the company purchased her from Alan Wheeler, restored her to military markings, coded her QJ-J (to honour Jeffrey Quill, their chief test pilot, who had been involved with the Spitfire since its earliest days and

In 1997 AB910 was dismantled at RAF Brize Norton and air-freighted across the Atlantic to take part in the United States Air Force anniversary celebrations. For this event she was marked as XR-A of 71 (Eagle) Squadron.
(Aeroplane Monthly Archive)

Flt Lt 'Merv' Paine at low level over Lincolnshire on the way home to RAF Coningsby. AB910 carries the codes XT-M of 603 Squadron.

Commemorating the man who designed her, AB910 is flown by Flt Lt Tim Nolan over the Somerset landscape on the way home from RNAS Culdrose in 1986.

AB910 is pushed into the hangar by the ground crew. She had been tasked to fly a display in the evening, but the crosswind dictated that the heavier Mk XIX would go instead. The Flight lays down very strict limits on the weather conditions in which the aircraft will fly. Safety is always uppermost in their minds, as well as the value and rarity of their charges. A limit of 5 knots of crosswind is laid down for all landings and take-offs and they do not operate at all in rain as this can severely damage the propeller blades.

Far left: The airscrew and cowling of AB910. She is at present painted in the desert colours of 244 Wing in Tunisia in 1943, as flown by Wg Cdr Ian 'Widge' Gleed.

Left: The cockpit of Spitfire Vb AB910. This is probably the most authentic interior of all the Spitfires owned by the Flight, even down to the spare bulb holder.

Above, left: A close-up of the markings currently applied to AB910.

Above, right: AB910, chocked front and back, and with the obligatory tool-kit in evidence. The white marking over the rim of the hub and the tyre is there to indicate any slippage between the tyre and the rim.

Right: Sqn Ldr Ian Smith is no stranger to the air-display circuit. He is in his second season with the Flight, but he has completed a tour with the Red Arrows as well as a year as manager for the Saudi Hawks team. AB910's desert camouflage makes her stand out nicely from the dark background of the Kielder Forest.

Wg Cdr 'Widge' Gleed AB910 carries the initials of Gleed (as opposed to the normal squadron codes) and also his personal insignia of 'Figaro the Cat'. Gleed was shot down in April 1943 in the vicinity of Cap Bon. His body was found some time later in the sand dunes.

had flown the prototype at Eastleigh), and flew her occasionally at displays.

On 16 September 1965 AB910 was flown to Coltishall by Jeffrey Quill and presented back to the Royal Air Force and the Flight on behalf of Vickers-Armstrong. In 1968, along with all the others, AB910 appeared in *The Battle of Britain* epic, wearing many different markings for this purpose.

This accident-prone machine was to have one more. On 27 October 1978 she was involved in a collision with a Harvard during a display at Bex in Switzerland. She sustained severe damage and was rebuilt at RAF Abingdon and RAF Kemble. At last, in October 1981, she rejoined the Flight at RAF Coningsby. In 1985 she was repainted at Cranfield as BP-O – the markings of one of five aircraft presented to the British by the American Research Foundation. In this guise she also carried below the cockpit the inscription 'In Memory of R.J. Mitchell'. Her American connections continued, as in 1997 she

was dismantled and shipped to America to take part in the United States Air Force anniversary celebrations. For this she was given 71 (Eagle) Squadron markings. At present AB910 has taken on the persona of the Spitfire V flown by Wg Cdr I.R. 'Widge' Gleed and appears in desert markings as applied in Tunisia in 1943.

The Spitfire IX is regarded by many as the best of 'the real Spitfires' – that is, those powered by the Merlin and not the Griffon engine. With its more powerful Merlin, a four-bladed airscrew and original-shaped fuselage and cockpit area, it is the ultimate development of the original beautiful design. The Spitfire IX owned by the Flight (MK356) was restored at RAF St Athan and test-flown by Sqn Ldr Paul Day in 1997, some fifty-three years after it had last been in the air.

Built at Castle Bromwich in 1944, the aircraft served with 443 (Hornet) Squadron RCAF in the ground-attack and fighter escort roles in the period leading up to the invasion of France. She has half an Me109 to her credit, and made three wheels-up landings, the last after losing a wheel on take-off. Despite this, her pilot continued with his mission, well knowing the problems he had to face on his return. After being repaired by a maintenance unit, MK356 was stored until the end of the war when she became a gate guardian, first at RAF Hawkinge and subsequently at RAF Locking. Even in her un-airworthy condition, she was pressed into service as a static airframe for *The Battle of Britain* film, after which she went to the museum at RAF St Athan. It was here that she was refurbished to airworthy condition, finished in the colours she had worn with 443 Squadron (21-V) and presented to the Flight.

Currently the Flight operates two Spitfire PR XIXs; these are two of the three original Mk XIXs (PM631, PS915 and PS853) that joined Hurricane LF363 at Biggin Hill in 1957 to form the Historic Aircraft Flight. PM631 has remained active with the Flight since that time, making her the longest serving of all aircraft on the Flight.

'Alone Above All' was the motto of 541 Squadron, which carried out high-altitude reconnaissance photography in the final year of the Second World War. This picture of the big, unarmed, Griffon-powered Spitfire gives a feeling of the space and solitude these aircraft were built to enjoy. Sqn Ldr Paul Day flies over the English Channel on the way home from Jersey in 1985.

In line astern for a circuit of Jersey before landing for the 1985 visit, Sqn Ldr Paul Day tucks in behind the Lancaster to enable the photographer to take advantage of some spectacular marine backgrounds. His aircraft is PM631, in the markings of a Mk XVI of 91 Squadron (coded DL-E). Note the heat haze from the exhaust stubs on the Spitfire.

Same day, just five minutes later, but the change in the weather makes this look very different from the preceding shot.

On the way to Fairford in 1986 Sqn Ldr Paul Day comes in close to the tail of the Hercules used by the Falcons parachute team. By organising transits of both groups to or from displays, we were able to use the Hercules without incurring extra hours on either the Battle of Britain Memorial Flight aircraft or the Hercules.

PM631 seen again from the ramp of a Hercules. The main disadvantage of this platform is the restricted angle of view caused by the exhaust trail from the Hercules, which dictates that one can only look down on the subject. If you go even slightly above the horizon, a blurred blob of exhaust smoke appears at the centre top of the image.

Spitfire PR XIX PS915 under complete rebuild by British Aerospace at Samlesbury in 1985. During this work she was modified to take a Griffon Mk 58 engine from a Shackleton. This required a redesign of the reduction gearbox to drive a single five-bladed propeller rather than the contra-rotating unit used by the Shackleton.

In 1985–6, with the enthusiastic support of the AOC 11 Group, the late Air Vice-Marshal Sir Ken Hayr, a display sequence was worked up for the Tornado F2 and the Spitfire XIX to appear as a duo. Sqn Ldr Paul Day was the Spitfire pilot with Wg Cdr Richard Peacock-Edwards driving the Tornado. Here, the two formate on the rear turret of the Lancaster on the way to their first public display at RAF Abingdon. With the Lancaster travelling at a comfortable 200 knots the Spitfire is quite happy but the Tornado is struggling. Its leading edge slats are deployed and it was using a great deal of up-elevator and power to remain in formation.

Opposite: PS853 was sold in June 1994 to defray the cost of rebuilding Hurricane LF363 after the crash at RAF Wittering. She is at present operated by Rolls-Royce and is based at Filton.

Left: The home team and visitors lined up outside the Battle of Britain Memorial Flight's headquarters at RAF Coningsby in the summer of 1986 to mark the last open day and display held there. Among the visitors can be seen the late Nick Grace refuelling his two-seat Spitfire V-OU, the Old Flying Machine Company's Mk IX (MH434), the Shuttleworth Collection's Mk Vc, and Spencer Flack's red Mk XVI, G-FIRE.

Spitfire PR XIX flown by Wg Cdr Paul Willis holds station off the port wing of the Lancaster over the English Channel. The trip to the Channel Islands is a return home for Paul, as he is a Guernsey man.

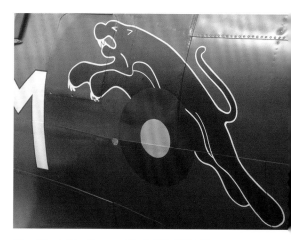

The Black Panther motif of 152 (SEAC) Squadron on PR XIX PS915.

PS915, flown by Wg Cdr Paul Willis, poses for a full-length shot. The distinctive curved windscreen of the Mk XIX is evident in this view.

PM631 was built at Southampton by Vickers-Armstrong (Supermarine) as part of a batch of 200 Mk VIII Spitfires, of which, after many changes of contract (Air/1877), 79 were finished as PR Mk XIXs. She was finally completed in November 1945, making her the only fighter operated by the Flight not to see wartime service. After initial storage at 6 MU at RAF Brize Norton, she was issued to 203 Advanced Flying School in May 1949. In January 1950 she returned to 6 MU and then on to RAF Cosford, where she stayed, apart from three weeks in Germany at Bucheburg, until she joined the Temperature and Humidity Meteorological Flight (THUM) at Woodvale in July 1951. She was operated by THUM until they re-equipped with

Mosquitos in June 1957, when, accompanied by the other two Mk XIXs, she was delivered back to the RAF at Duxford.

Since then, she has moved to every new home with the Flight, took part in the fly-past with LF363 at Sir Winston Churchill's interment, played the obligatory role in *The Battle of Britain* film and in 1964 took part in an air-to-air combat sortie with a Gloster Javelin to assess the use of Firestreak missiles against piston-engined aircraft. This last event was carried out on behalf of 60 Squadron, which was equipped with Javelins in the Far East during the Indonesian crisis.

PM631 has appeared with the Flight in the markings of 11 and 91 Squadrons, and after a major service in the winter of 2001–2 emerged in the PRU

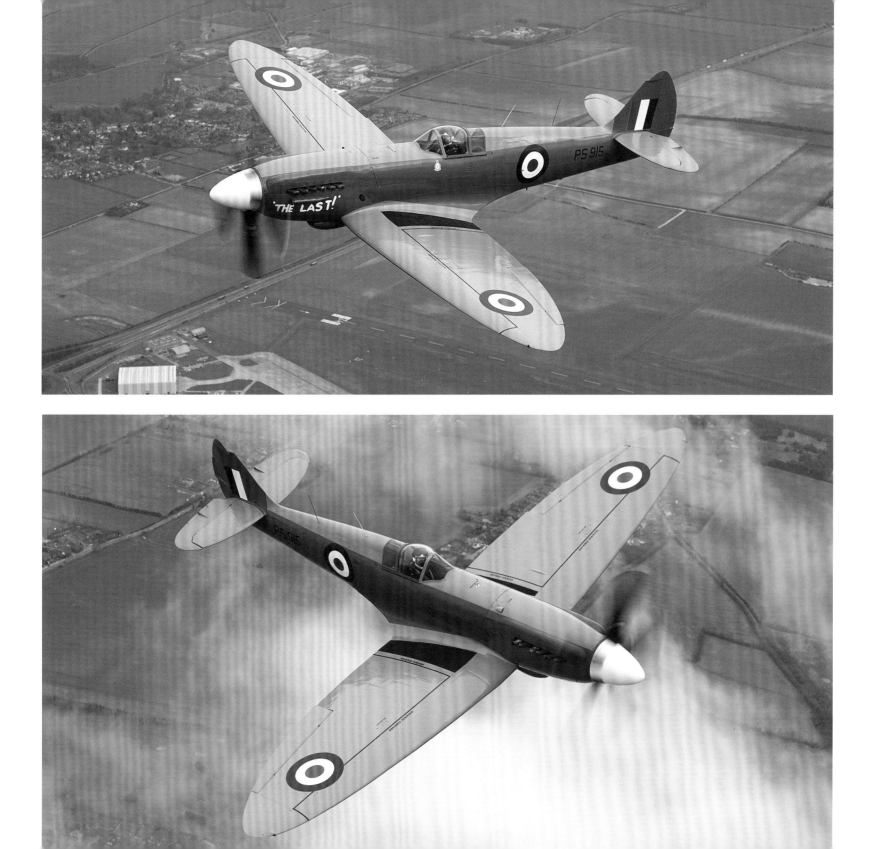

blue scheme of an early Mk XIX belonging to 541 Squadron, which was one of several squadrons responsible for high-altitude photo-reconnaissance over Europe during the last year of the Second World War.

Spitfire PS915 was part of the same batch of Mk VIIIs finished as Mk XIXs as PM631. Built at Southampton, she was delivered to 6 MU at RAF Brize Norton in April 1945. From here she was issued to the Central Photographic Reconnaissance Unit at RAF Benson. After two months with this unit she was allocated to 541 Squadron, where she spent a year before returning to RAF Benson. She stayed here for only three months before moving to 151 Photographic Reconnaissance Unit, where she remained until July 1948, when she joined 2 Squadron in Germany. In 1949 she suffered a serious accident and after lengthy repairs and a period in storage she was issued to the THUM Flight as a replacement aircraft for PM631.

Spitfire PR Mk XIX, PS915, flown by Sqn Ldr Clive Rowley, photographed during her transit flight from Duxford to Coningsby after her major overhaul at the beginning of 2004. During this work she was given the markings of PR XIX PS888 from 81 Squadron based at Seletar in Singapore, which flew the last ever operational sortie by a Spitfire in 1954. For this mission the legend 'The Last!' was emblazoned on her port cowling.

PS915 joined the Flight with PM631 and PS853, but her stay was short-lived as she was allocated to RAF West Malling for ground display duties in August 1957. Subsequently she was put on gate guardian duties at RAF Leuchars and then at RAF Brawdy. Unlike most gate guardians, which are left to the mercies of wind and weather, she was well looked after at Brawdy, even being given an indoor billet during the winter months! As a result of this care she was still in reasonable condition when it was decided to restore her to flying condition. Sir Ken Hayr, AOC 11 Group and always a keen supporter of the Flight, was one of the prime movers in getting her to British Aerospace at Samlesbury where she was completely refurbished and modified to take a Griffon engine from a Shackleton.

Close-up details of the Spitfire IX MK356. This finish is reasonably well worn, making her look far more like an operational machine.

PS915 returned to the Flight in 1987, and has since masqueraded as a Mk XIV to commemorate the work carried out by test pilots of both Supermarine and A&AEE at Boscombe Down. She also spent some time, still in the guise of a Mk XIV, in the markings of an aircraft operated by 152 (SEAC) Squadron. At present she is resplendent in a PRU blue and grey colour scheme with the slogan 'The Last' emblazoned on her cowling. This represents PR Mk XIX PS888, which made the last RAF operational flight of a Spitfire from RAF Seletar, Singapore, in 1954.

The third Spitfire XIX, PS853, joined the Flight in 1957. Its history was similar to that of the other two. After service with the THUM Flight and a period as gate guardian, she finally rejoined the Flight in 1964. In 1994 she was sold to cover the cost of rebuilding Hurricane LF363, and is at present owned and operated by Rolls-Royce, based at Filton.

Sqn Ldr Clive Rowley gets up close to the rear turret of the Lancaster in MK356. This aircraft wears the markings it carried during its time with 443 (Hornet) Squadron RCAF. Flown by Flg Off Gordon Ockenden, on D-Day plus one it helped provide air cover for the invasion beach-head. MK356 is fitted with a Merlin 66 engine, optimised for operation at low level, and also has clipped wings to increase the rate of roll at low altitude.

MK356, flown by Sqn Ldr Clive Rowley, viewed from the rear turret of the Lancaster. These views emphasise the lack of a straight line anywhere on the aircraft, while the head-on shot illustrates the under-stated gull wing.

Opposite: Clive Rowley in the Flight's Spitfire Mk IX gets close in to the rear turret of the Lancaster on the way to Great Yarmouth.

CHAPTER 6

The Douglas DC-3 Dakota – ZA947

The Douglas Dakota, of which nearly 11,000 were built, is the military variant of the highly successful DC-3 airliner. Some 2,000 of these aeroplanes were used by the RAF in transport and supply roles from 1941, when the RAF took delivery of their first twelve aircraft, until 1970, when the final 'Dak' was retired from service.

The Flight's Dakota, ZA947, succeeded its De Havilland Devon as the main support, transport and continuation training aircraft in 1993. She was built in 1942 and was operated by the USAAF and RCAF before being declared surplus to requirements in 1971. She was then purchased by the Royal Aircraft Establishment (RAE) at Farnborough, where she was used in tests for dropping sonar buoys and launching remotely piloted vehicles (RPVs). For this work holes were cut in the fuselage, which needed to be repaired to return her to her original configuration. Indeed, a great deal of work has been carried out on her to restore her to 'as-built' condition. She has now been fully fitted with para-seats and has been used in that role at commemorative events over the past few years.

The Dak is used to transport both aircrew and ground crew to various events, along with any spares and tools that may be needed. She is also used as a continuation trainer for the Lancaster crews during the winter months when that aircraft is unavailable due to essential maintenance. In addition, she has become a display aircraft in her own right and is seen at displays throughout the country, either in the company of a Spitfire and a Hurricane or as a singleton. Currently she is in the markings of 267 'Pegasus' Squadron, which during 1943 and 1944 operated in the Middle East in the special operations role, dropping partisans behind enemy lines.

Junior Technician Jack Dempsey (Engine Technician) replaces spark plugs on the Flight's Dakota.

Opposite, top: It's 15 January 2007 and the Dak with Sqn Ldr Stu Reid and Flt Lt Ed Straw at the controls finds the only patch of sunlight over Lincolnshire. The winter of 2006–7 was one of the wettest and windiest on record which put paid to most flying activity. This was about the fifth attempt to get this picture.

Opposite, bottom: The Dak is refuelled at Barkston Heath where the Flight was based while the runway at Coningsby was being re-surfaced and before the arrival of the Eurofighter Typhoon.

Above: A glimmer of light through the overcast sky gives a period feel to this image. The face at the window is that of Flt Lt Jack Hawkins, the Flight's Adjutant and Operations Officer.

Above: The dragon-like nose of the Dak shows the Pegasus emblem of 267 Squadron. She is finished in the colours worn by the squadron while operating in the supply role to partisans in 1943–4.

Below: 'Rosie's Nightmare' – thousands of rivets in very close formation. The fact that these aircraft during their service life were to a great extent expendable is evident by the very basic construction seen in this view of the Dak. Its very simplicity though was much of the reason for its success both as a war horse and a commercial aircraft.

The Dak taxies at States Airport, Jersey, as the Flight arrives for the annual Battle of Britain display.

Above: Here is another close-up of the markings of 267 Squadron.

Above right: A myriad of rivets emphasising the well-used look that gives the Dak its distinctive patina.

Right: A Pratt and Whitney Twin Wasp engine, fresh from overhaul, awaits installation in the Flight's Dak.

Below: While away at displays during the summer, the ground crew spend much of the time on the ground cleaning oil from the engines and the airframe of the Dak. Here Cpl Norman Pringle gets to grips with keeping the Dak in pristine condition. By the state of the fuselage in the background it would appear to be an uphill slog.

CHAPTER 7
The Aircrew

The primary aim of the Battle of Britain Memorial Flight is to preserve the aircraft in its care in an airworthy condition as a flying memorial to those who flew them in anger during the Second World War and who, in many cases, gave their lives while doing so. The men who fly these aircraft today are entrusted with a most important part of the nation's heritage.

Aircrew for the Flight are drawn from all areas of the RAF, many from fighter squadrons, some from Hercules units, some from the AWACS unit at Waddington and some even from helicopter units. The tradition of the Commanding Officer being the Lancaster 'driver' has passed and the present incumbent, Sqn Ldr Al Pinner MBE, is typical in that his experience in the air force has been mainly with the Harrier, in which type he has seen active service both in the Balkans and in the Middle East. He has also spent time with the Canadian Air Force flying the CF-18. Al spent four years with the Flight under the watchful eye of the previous Commanding Officer, Sqn Ldr Clive Rowley, building up his experience on the fighters and learning the operating procedures of the Flight before taking over his present post. In common with almost all the aircrew, this four-year period was on a voluntary basis as all aircrew have a 'day job' in the Air Force and devote most of their free time (especially in the summer, when there are displays every weekend and usually a couple of days in the week as well) to fly the Flight's aircraft. By the end of a busy display season one does hear the odd remark about having some time off!

The DHC-1 Chipmunk has served for many years with the Flight as a continuation trainer, and in these days of jet training from the start in the RAF, it is a way of initiating would-be pilots for the Flight into the very different world of handling piston-engined tail-wheel aircraft. The Flight operates two of these delightful aircraft which, in addition to the training role, are also used for general 'hack' duties as well as the reconnaissance of new display sites. They are the last of the type to be operated by the RAF and are finished in a smart high complicity black scheme. WK518 is being flown here by Sqn Ldr 'Shiney' Simmons.

In days gone by, when the RAF still operated the Shackleton and Hastings, training for the supercharged heavy piston role in the Flight was a somewhat easier matter than it is today, and the sourcing of aircrew with relevant experience was simpler too. The Lancaster crew could be recruited from a squadron whose aircraft demanded similar handling techniques to those of the Lancaster, and continuation training was a matter of a trip to Lossiemouth to put in a few hours on a Shackleton from 8 Squadron. The connection with 8 Squadron is still maintained as they are now based 'just up the road' from Coningsby at RAF Waddington, where they operate Boeing E-3 AWACS aircraft. Three of the Lancaster crew, including Bomber Leader Sqn Ldr Stuart Reid, are pilots with 8 Squadron.

The navigators for the bomber all come from a background of fast jet operation. Some have display experience, others have not, but all offer the professionalism and commitment that are essential to the smooth running of the Flight. Similarly experienced are the flight engineers and loadmasters. The flight engineers are drawn from AWACS, Hercules or training backgrounds, while the loadmasters have all had combat experience with various Hercules squadrons based at RAF Lyneham.

The Flight's pilots do not set out to push the outer limits of the performance envelope of any of the aircraft; rather they display their charges in a manner that shows off their individual lines and also gives the crowd the chance to hear the unmistakable song of the Rolls-Royce Merlin. The aircraft are so

Pre-flight walk-around checks are carried out by both the pilot and the flight engineer. Here, Flight Engineer Flt Sgt Andy Beacham with his magic wand consults Cpl Mark Arnold, who is connecting his headset to the communications plug inside the port wheel-well. This allows him full communication with the aircrew during the start sequence.

precious that certain rules regarding the weather are always applied and are rigidly adhered to. This can give rise to disappointment when the aircraft fail to make their scheduled appearance at a display. For this reason alone it is worth explaining more about these self-imposed rules.

One of the most limiting of the elements is the wind. For safe operation the wind speed must not exceed 25 knots and the crosswind component of the wind affecting the runway from which the aircraft are to operate must not exceed 15 knots for take-off and 10 knots for landing. Compared with the fighters of today, these aircraft are light, and even former Second World War Spitfire pilots would admit that the aircraft could be skittish, to say the least, in any form of crosswind. If the Flight were to operate out of 'old-fashioned' airfields with their choice of runway directions, or off grass fields where one has 360 degrees of choice, rather than in the

main from modern, single runway NATO or commercial runways that take less heed of wind direction, life would certainly be easier.

Another governing factor linked to this imposed limit is the relative lack of experience most of the RAF's pilots have in piston-engined tail-wheel aircraft. This is not to decry their aviation skills, but flying one of these venerable aeroplanes is a completely different ball-game from their everyday job in the world of fast jets. Putting one of these machines safely back on the ground again in one piece requires skills that are no longer taught in today's Air Force.

General weather limitations are just as strict, the requirements being a cloud-base no lower than 1,500 feet and visibility of 5 km. When you stop to think about this, though, they are very realistic. Apart from the addition of modern radio equipment, the instrumentation in all the Flight's aircraft is essentially the same as when they were operational. The Lancaster and the Dakota boast satellite navigational aids, but in all the fighters the navigation is by OS map and stop-watch! Given that many of the displays are not held at major venues, these general weather limitations begin to seem very sensible.

I was once in the Lancaster during a sortie to carry out three fly-pasts at events local to RAF Coningsby. One of them was at Louth, where we discovered on arrival that there were two separate events on opposite sides of the town. Instantly the decision was made to change the approach line, thus taking in both shows at no extra cost! There are also apocryphal stories of displays being flown for one man and his dog in a field, while a mile away the assembled crowd, although slightly disappointed by the distance of the aircraft, were quite satisfied and pleased to see them!

Rainfall comes within the general weather limitations. The aircraft are not deliberately flown in precipitation of any sort because of the damage that can be caused to the airframe and especially the propeller blades. The propeller blades on the fighters are of laminated wooden construction with a plasticised finish. This is the original specification for the aircraft and also has the advantage of lessening the risk of serious airframe damage and shock loading to the Merlin engine in the unlikely event of a wheels-up landing having to be made. The propeller, in flight, is turning at some 2,500rpm and is being pulled through the air at some 200mph, so you don't need a degree in science to realise the abrasive effect precipitation will have on the surface of the propeller blades. Once the surface coating is stripped away the laminations of the core begin to separate. Given that each blade costs a four-figure

Lancaster PA474 formates on the Andover used by the RAF Falcons parachute team over the sun-dappled countryside of Cambridgeshire. She is being flown by Sqn Ldr Tony Banfield.

'The Major', Sqn Ldr Paul Day OBE, AFC, waits on the wing of AB910 to get airborne from Barkston Heath.

sum, you can begin to see the reasoning behind this further limitation!

These are the reasons behind the occasional 'no show' at a display. There are, however, further self-imposed limits laid down for the actual display of the aircraft. Some private owners are inclined to 'wring out' their machines and the temptation to do this in something as powerful and responsive as a Spitfire or Hurricane must be enormous. The Battle of Britain Flight, however, adopts the attitude that, while they are there to display the aircraft to the public, they do so as custodians of an important part of the country's history. Therefore the following constraints are imposed: maximum indicated air speed does not exceed 275 knots, with maximum boost for the Merlins being +6 while the Griffons are allowed +7. Minimum height during the display is 100ft, with a limit of +3g and -0g – the latter restriction is imposed to lessen the airframe fatigue factor and is also due to the fact that neither the Spitfire nor the Hurricanes are fitted with inverted fuel systems. These constraints limit the display routine to the vertical axis (loops, etc.) and dictate that the display consists of a gentle series of turns and wing-overs orientated along the display line to give the crowd the best view of the aircraft.

Having got the limitations out of the way, we come next to the actual planning of the transit flights to and from the destination and the actual display. The route taken usually follows the shortest distance between the two relevant points, in order to conserve valuable hours on the aeroplanes. In general this works, but other factors always need to be taken into account. For example, in poor weather the Pennines may be off limits, or perhaps Heathrow air traffic control cannot allow the Flight through its zone. The planning for each trip is carried out a good few days in advance of the sortie so that any problems can be sorted in good time. If the venue for the display is one that has not been flown before and appears to present problems of any sort, one of the Chipmunks may well be used to carry out a reconnaissance of the site. Quite often the Flight attends a show as a three-ship formation – the Lancaster, a Spitfire and a Hurricane – and if this is the case then the fighters transit in formation with the bomber, whose navigator is responsible for the whole formation. The fighter pilots, however, still work out the course for themselves in case the bomber has to abort for any reason or even fails to go at all. In the event of either of the fighters being unserviceable, there is usually a back-up aircraft available (unless there are requirements for fighter attendance at other venues). In the event of the weather being unkind, transit routes may have to be changed and in rare cases, if four or five venues are due to be attended, one may have to be dropped from the programme to ensure appearance at all the others. Often the Flight is away for a few days at a time, for example when visiting the International Air Tattoos at Fairford during which time the weather may change completely, necessitating the redrawing of routes. This is when individual maps begin to look as if they have been drawn by spiders!

It is usually when they are at the furthest distance from home that things go wrong with aircraft! The visit to the Isle of Man in 2002 is a good example. This event was attended by the Dakota, Spitfire XIX PS915 and Hurricane PZ865. I went to the Isle of Man to link up with the Flight for the purpose of carrying out air-to-air photography of the fighters from the Dakota on the transit home to RAF Coningsby. While I was waiting at the airport to meet up with the ground crew, the fighters arrived from the display venue in the north of the island. The weather was dull but within limits, and it was only after the Spitfire had completed three circuits that we realised something was wrong. The undercarriage was locked in the retracted position! The pilot flew round for about half an hour, to burn off fuel in case he had to perform a wheels-up landing, and then took the aeroplane to about 4,000 feet to carry out some negative 'g' manoeuvres in the hope that this would free the locking mechanism. The ploy worked and within minutes the aeroplane was safe on the runway. In the meantime, however, the Hurricane had landed but was being held on the taxi-way with its engine running, to await the arrival of the Spitfire. The cooling system on these aircraft is designed for use in the air and not for prolonged operation on the ground. Because the Hurricane had been held by Air Traffic Control for a good 20 minutes, its radiator expired. The radiator on the Hurricane is at least more conveniently placed than that on the Spitfire, being in the airflow from the propeller. On the Merlin-engined Spitfire the radiators are so placed as to have no benefit from the propeller and if the Spitfires are not airborne within 6 or 7 minutes from start-up they are in real danger of overheating.

So there we all were on the Isle of Man with two unserviceable aircraft. The Spitfire needed a new hydraulic pump and the Hurricane a new radiator. We all flew home in the Dakota together with the 'dead' radiator removed from the Hurricane, leaving both fighters on the island. Hurricane radiators are not a 'shelf item' and the unit taken from PZ865 had to be sent away for repair before being taken back to the island and refitted. All this took two aircraft and three ground crew away from the Flight for nearly ten days, causing much replanning and extra hours on the remaining fighters.

The British weather can turn the best-laid plans into a nightmare, or at least present problems that need to be solved instantly to ensure that commitments can be fulfilled while operating well within the safety parameters laid down by the Flight. A case in point was the trip made to RAF Leuchars in July 2006. It was an opportunity for me to do some photography during the transit from Coningsby

Amid a cloud of smoke, Al Pinner gets PS915 started up for an evening trip to Shrivenham. The Mk XIX Spitfires have now all been converted from Coffman cartridge starters to electric. This is a far more reliable system, especially with a hot engine.

using the scenery over the Scottish Borders and the Firth of Forth as a background. At RAF Coningsby the day dawned bright but the Met people were telling us that there was fog and low cloud at Leuchars and that at Carlisle, the alternative airfield, the cross-wind was out of limits. Tees-side was proposed as an alternative but as they had their own air display that day, the controllers there were understandably not that keen to have extra aircraft movements that might interfere with their schedule. It was therefore decided to transit to Edinburgh and operate from there. As well as doing away with the beautiful backgrounds I was looking forward to, the whole trip needed to be replanned from the Flight's

point of view, including organising hotel accommodation in Edinburgh, which in the week before the Festival is not the easiest of tasks! Nevertheless it was all achieved in the end. I ended up with the pictures I wanted and the Flight's obligations were duly fulfilled.

For the Lancaster, the same limits are imposed as far as weather, flight levels and stress factors are concerned and planning has to take place in the same way. The main difference is that the bomber has a dedicated navigator. This member of the crew is a specialist in his day job as a navigator in Tornados, AWACS or Dominies, where he is up to date with all the latest computerised equipment.

Although the Lancaster does carry a GPS unit, all navigation is again by map and stop-watch. Everything happens much more slowly in the Lancaster than in a fast jet, and it is possible for the navigator to get ahead of himself! Added to this, of course, is the need for precision timing at displays. If the Flight is due to cross the hedge at a particular event at a particular time, then this is exactly what has to happen – to the second – or the navigator is inevitably told by the pilot on the intercom exactly how many seconds early or late he is. Certainly this is a steep learning curve for newcomers.

The navigator isn't the only crew member to face a steep learning curve. Since the demise of the Avro Shackletons of 8 Squadron for crew training on supercharged piston multi-engined aircraft, the pilots' learning curve is almost at the vertical. Most of the Lancaster aircrew have no first-hand experience at all when they arrive at the Flight. The closest thing to a Shackleton in today's air force is a Hercules, the 'driving' of which is an altogether different experience. Crew training is carried out on the Dakota, the crewmen 'serving their time' in this aircraft before becoming co-pilot in the Lancaster and finally its Captain.

Sqn Ldr Paul Day flies PS915 over the Channel.

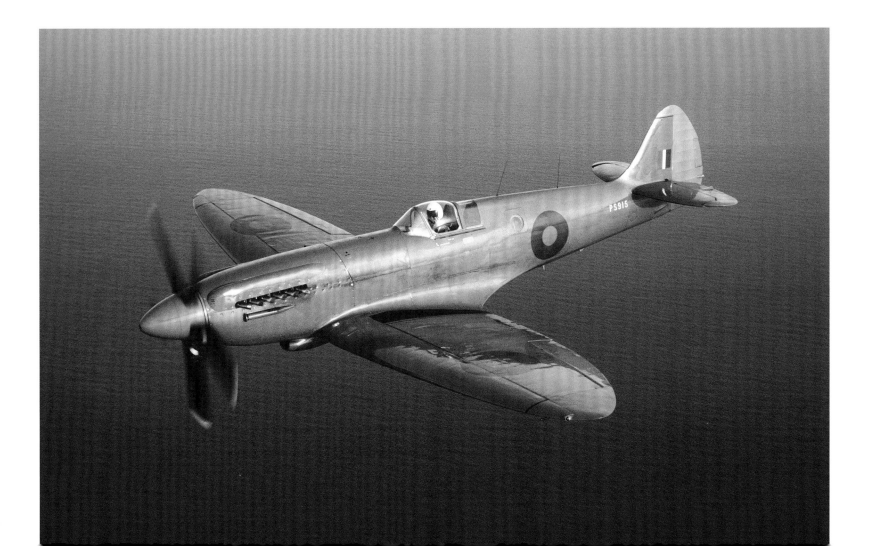

CHAPTER 8

The Ground Crew

The Flight has four administrative staff: Flt Lt 'Jack' Hawkins, who joined in 1998 as Adjutant (having flown Shackletons, Vulcans and Nimrods), and his team Jeanette O'Connell, Di Holland and Jim Stewart. They are the Flight's first line of defence, fielding all initial enquiries, and they are responsible for the smooth day-to-day running of the Flight, as well as organising aircrew currency, hotel accommodation, road management, and so on. They also answer enquiries, support public speaking engagements, fend off people like me and generally do anything that no one else wants to do. Jack has recently been awarded a Commander-in-Chief Strike Command's Commendation for his services to the Flight.

The Flight now operates eleven aircraft, which are maintained by twenty-three permanent mechanics and technicians. The permanency of this group is a relatively new situation for the Flight, as for many years ground crew were seconded to the Battle of Britain Flight, their everyday job in the Air Force taking precedence in case of emergency or shortage on their appointed section. Even then they would work all night and at weekends if necessary to keep the aircraft serviceable. They still do work all night on occasions, but at least they are going to be working from day to day! In addition to this group

of technicians there are two suppliers who organise the ordering and procurement of the multitude of various spares that have to be obtained. There are also three safety equipment personnel who look after the supply and servicing of flying equipment and clothing.

I think it is fair to say that the ground crew are the most important part of the whole organisation. The pilots and aircrew get all the glory, but without the ground crew there would be no glory to be had! There is a very definite feeling on the Flight that the ground crew 'own' the aircraft, and woe betide anyone who treats a machine harshly or returns it in a less than pristine condition.

There are no longer organised training facilities to teach newcomers to the Flight the foibles and intricacies of these airframes or the engines that power them, so all training is undertaken on the job where the experience gained over the years is handed on to the 'new faces'. Given that anyone joining will have a good grounding in the first place, it is generally found that within nine months the newcomer will know enough to work without close supervision. These days however it has become more and more probable that newcomers to the Flight may well never have dealt with piston engines or basic airframes. Therefore the premise has been

TOOL BOARD A

This tool-board is in the hangar at Coningsby. A system of individually numbered discs that replace tools in use is utilised so that all tools are traceable.

Below, left: Chief Technician Paul Blackah spends a great deal of his spare time painstakingly restoring a Spitfire XVI, TE311. This aircraft, along with another Mk XVI, TB382, was allocated to the Flight in 2002 and struck off charge. TE311 has since become part of a 'spares recovery' project.

Below, right: Junior Technician Neil Clegg refuels Hurricane LF363. These are the tanks that were originally fitted when the wing cannon were removed early in her life. Neil Clegg served with the Red Arrows for two-and-a-half years before joining the Battle of Britain Memorial Flight in 2001. He left the Flight in 2003 for a posting to RAF Cottesmore, returning in 2005 for his second tour with them. There is great rivalry between the two display teams and Clegg pays every day for his association with the BBMF's rivals, but he puts up with the ribbing in a pretty stoical fashion. He is also a keen and able photographer and, along with Chief Technician Keith Brenchley, he supplies many of the photographs used in the Flight's annual brochure.

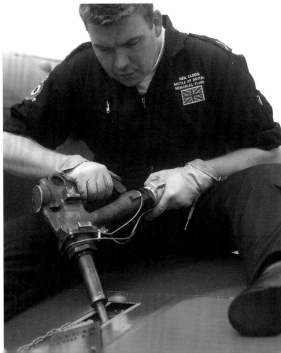

adopted that 'nothing trains you for service in the BBMF like working in the BBMF!', and the traditional on-the-job training has been formalised.

The engineering year at the Flight can be divided into two distinct sections. The winter period between October and the end of March is when the major servicing is carried out. During this period the aircraft are thoroughly inspected, replacement parts obtained (and in some cases manufactured) to replace those that are worn or are known to be near the end of their lives, electrical systems are checked and radio equipment is removed and serviced.

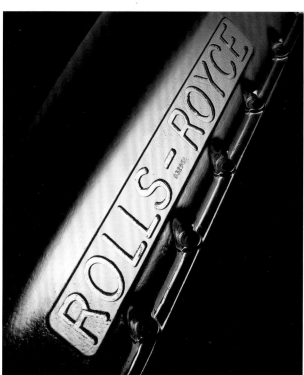

Opposite: Spitfire PR XIX PS915 with Hawker Hurricane IIc PZ865 off the Needles on their way to the Channel Islands for the annual Battle of Britain display. The Spitfire is flown by Wg Cdr Paul Willis and the Hurricane by Sqn Ldr 'Shiney' Simmons.

Left: The main workshop at Retro Track and Air, with Merlin and Griffon engines being assembled.

Far left: The rocker cover on a Merlin.

Left: The quality of the workmanship is evident in the finish on this supercharger fan.

Undercarriage retraction tests are carried out and ground-running of engines is undertaken. Some Merlins or Griffons may have to be removed and sent away for either major or minor overhaul and checking. Also during this time the propellers are inspected and if needs be sent away to Dowty-Rotol for refurbishing.

The summer servicing schedule is confined to everyday checks and the replacement of items that unexpectedly become unserviceable. Due to the limitations imposed on the operational envelope of these aircraft, the time lapse between major services has been doubled compared to that which applied when the aeroplanes were operational!

The technicians are split into several groups. The engineers are headed by Warrant Officer Dick Harmer, who is in charge of the whole engineering and maintenance unit. He has been in the RAF for forty years and his experience of a large range of piston- and jet-engined aircraft is invaluable. Chief Technician Paul Blackah has nearly thirty years' service and is similarly experienced. Paul has almost single-handedly taken on the rebuild, section by section, of the Spitfire XVI that arrived at Coningsby in April 2002, having been used for many years as a ground display airframe by the Exhibition Flight. This he is doing during his lunch hours and in any spare time that comes his way. He is no stranger to this work as, together with Russ Snadden, he was responsible for the rebuilding to airworthy status of the Messerschmitt Bf109G 'Black Six', all the while maintaining his normal RAF day job! Sgt Mark Arnold has now returned to the Flight as Engineering Controller after a sojourn at Cottesmore working on the Harrier GR7/7As of 3 (F) and 4 (AC) Squadrons.

Below, left: An overhead cam and rocker assembly – the whole thing just speaks of quality!

Below, right: The top end of a connecting rod ready to be assembled – this could easily be a piece of jewellery, so exquisite is the finish!

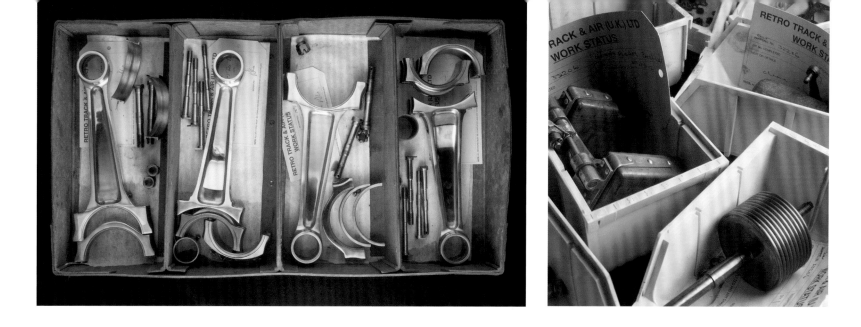

Chief Technician Keith Brenchley and Corporal Nigel Bunn are the longest serving members of the propulsion unit, having twenty-six years' experience on the Flight between them. Keith is in charge of this section and in 2002 became a full-time reservist. He

Above: The stroke on a Griffon crankshaft is checked for wear. Polishing techniques adopted from the 'track' side of the business have been adopted and adapted for use with aero-engines with excellent results.

is, in addition to his engineering skills, an accomplished photographer and has been responsible for many of the illustrations used in the annual brochure produced by the Flight. His work also graces the pages of some of the leading aviation journals. Nigel Bunn came to Coningsby fifteen years ago straight from a tour with 8 Squadron operating Shackletons, and has the obvious advantage of familiarity with the type's Griffon engine. Bunn is also a full-time reservist. Sgt Mark Arnold, at present on his second tour of duty with the Flight, has been with the Flight for five years after tours at Lossiemouth, Honington, Wattisham and Bruggen, all as an engine technician on Tornados. The rest of the crew – Cpl Dave Ford, Junior Technician (JT) Mark Kirkpatrick, JT Wes Martin, JT Leigh Poiner and JT Mark Thompson – have an average of three years' service with the Battle of Britain Memorial Flight. In a few years time I am sure that a couple of these newcomers will have wangled their way to a more senior position with the Flight. If forced to leave, such men are tracked for a possible quick return to the Flight. These members of the ground crew look after the Merlin and Griffon engines, carry out general servicing and change engines when needs be.

Above, left: When an engine is dismantled into its sub-assemblies, all the components are stored and labelled prior to inspection, non-destructive testing and cleaning, or replacing for reassembly. Here, connecting rods with their bearing shells and caps await inspection.

Above, right: Some of the components of a carburettor wait to be cleaned. In front is the barometric device that automatically allows more air to be fed into the fuel mixture as the aircraft gains height. To the left are the floats from the float chamber, which are made of varnished cork.

Right: Retro has built its own test-rig for Merlin and Griffon engines and is able to transport engines to nearby Kemble airfield, close to Cirencester, for trial running. I for one can vouch for the fact that when the engines are run up to full power, one feels rather than hears the noise!

Below, left and right: The Spitfire is stripped back to bare metal before priming and painting begin. Seeing the airframe in this condition emphasises the delicacy of the design. Camouflage makes it appear a great deal heavier and bulkier.

The Airframe Technicians are led by their Trade Manager CT Paul Blackah. He and his team – Cpl Neil Clegg, Cpl Mark Crosby, Cpl Norman Pringle, JT Chris Elcock, JT Rachel Warnes, SAC Mark Barlow and SAC Jodie Fox – are responsible, as their designation makes clear, for the structure and fabric of the aircraft. They are also responsible for the pre-flight preparation of the aircraft, refuelling, cleaning the airframes, and so on. For a small team of eight, this is a more than full-time occupation and for this reason they are unable to take on the more time-consuming work of deep servicing or stripping and respraying. The aircraft are resprayed in new markings every four or five years, which requires them to be stripped back to bare metal before being primed and sprayed. In the past the aircraft were finished in gloss paint to facilitate cleaning and to give better durability. However, new matt finish paints are being used as they offer sufficient protection and are a more authentic representation of the original.

The five members of the specialist Electrical and Avionics team are responsible for solving all the electrical problems peculiar to the aircraft. Led by Sgt Ian Davies, they are Cpl Andy Bale, Cpl Craig Facey, JT James Walker and SAC Darren Critten. Compared to the training this team have had on aircraft such as the Tornado, Harrier or Jaguar, their charges at the Flight are basic to say the least. Ignition harnesses and basic radio equipment take the place of computer electronics!

The Suppliers and Safety Equipment Fitters, Sgt Steve Main, Cpl Richie Lloyd, Cpl Gary Taylor, SAC Becky Dowsing and SAC Carl Davis are responsible not only for the fitting and maintenance of all flying clothing and equipment, but also for the procurement and storage of all aircraft spares. The aircrew are required to wear state-of-the-art flying helmets that not only can be life savers but also contain sophisticated electronics for communications. These have to be checked and serviced on a regular basis so an intimate knowledge of

Stripped and primed. The stripped condition of this engine cowling panel emphasises the hand-built character of the aircraft. It is interesting how even a coat of primer tends to make the whole thing look a great deal more 'professional'.

Clive Denney, looking like a cross between a Bedouin and an astronaut, applies one of the fuselage roundels to AB910. The research into correct colours is long and painstaking – and often confusing. In the case of the chosen markings for this aircraft, there are different schools of thought as to which exact colours were used on the original. Just like a large model aeroplane, AB910 is masked off with tape and brown paper.

communications electronics is required by this team. Procurement of spares for modern aircraft is a matter of filling in the appropriate form and waiting for delivery. With the aircraft of the Battle of Britain Memorial Flight, however, it can be a case of a lengthy search, involving private owners both in this country and abroad, as spare parts become more difficult to source. In turn, private owners often seek help and advice from the Flight, whose members are, if able, always willing to help. The Flight has held for many years vast quantities of spares that until recently remained uncatalogued and were stored in less than ideal conditions. Thanks to a great deal of hard work these have been properly organised and

engineers can now see at a glance what is readily available. The Flight also enjoys the full support of BAe Systems, which can usually help if spares have to be manufactured from scratch. Some spares are manufactured by fitters at maintenance units within the RAF, often at short notice, to enable an aircraft to remain airworthy during the display season.

This 'extended family' that is responsible for the upkeep of the Flight's aircraft really is the core of the whole operation. Their devotion and dedication are extraordinary. It is, however, very much the case that the aeroplanes belong to the engineers first and the country second, and they are let out to the aircrew to be flown and displayed. Long may it remain so!

Clive Denny puts the
finishing touches to 'Figaro
the Cat'.

The Lancaster, flown by Sqn Ldr 'Scott' Anderson, accompanied by Paul Day in the Spitfire PR Mk XIX, and Merv Paine in the Hurricane, transit to Guernsey from Jersey for the Battle of Britain Air Display.